Digitizing Your Family History

RHONDA R. McCLURE

Digitizing
Your Family History

Easy methods

for preserving your

heirloom documents,

photos, home movies,

and more in a digital format.

PETITION FOR NATURALIZATION

baby's first footprints

FAMILY TREE BOOKS

CINCINNATI, OHIO

www.familytreemagazine.com

Other fine Family Tree Books are available from your local bookstore or on our Web site at www.familytreemagazine.com.

08   07   06   05   04   5   4   3   2   1

Library of Congress Cataloging-in-Publication Data

McClure, Rhonda R.
   Digitizing your family history : easy methods for preserving your heirloom documents, photos, home movies and more in a digital format / Rhonda R. McClure—1st ed.
     p. cm.
   Includes bibliographical references and index.
   ISBN 1-55870-708-5
   1. Genealogy—Computer network resources. Digital preservation. I. Title.
CS21.M33   2004
929′.1′028516—dc22   2004050645
                                                   CIP

Editor: Sharon DeBartolo Carmack, CG
Associate editor: Erin Nevius
Production coordinator: Robin Richie
Interior designer: Sandy Conopeotis Kent
Cover design by Nick Gliebe of Design Matters
Icon designer: Cindy Beckmeyer

About the Author

Rhonda R. McClure is a professional genealogical researcher, lecturer, and author. She has been involved in research for twenty years, and has spent the last fifteen years using online genealogy to facilitate and enhance her research endeavors. While she began her genealogical research before computers, she embraced the technology early on and continues to welcome the new methods and features made available through the ever-changing field of computers. She has written extensively for a variety of genealogical periodicals. This is her ninth book and her third for Family Tree Books. She lectures frequently around the country, applying the digitizing of photos and documents to enhance her lecture presentations.

DEDICATION

For Myra, who continues to see more in me than I see in myself.

Acknowledgments

An author may have a concept for a book, but it is through the input, guidance, advice, and sharing of information by many others that the final manuscript eventually becomes a book. And I want to thank those who offered their help and support with this latest project. It was a wonderful writing experience.

To those at Family Tree Books who accepted the vision of this work and gave it the green light, thank you. To Sharon DeBartolo Carmack, thank you for time, input, and understanding as this project progressed. Erin Nevius, your guidance and willingness to listen is always appreciated, as is your friendship.

Special thanks to Bruce Buzbee for his constant willingness to let me use screen shots of his wonderful genealogy program, RootsMagic. My heartfelt thanks to Gordon Nuttall of Hewlett Packard for his consideration at HPWorld 2003 in taking time during a busy conference to listen to an insignificant individual's project and see the potential in the products his company develops. He answered many questions for me about upcoming products, some of which at the time were not available yet in the United States. Thanks to Maureen Taylor for her willingness to share that wonderful daguerreotype with me.

No one can accomplish much without the support of friends and family, and I am no exception. Michael LeClerc, thank you for your support, your nagging, your jokes, and your Macintosh knowledge. I count myself lucky to call you a friend. To Paula Stuart Warren, our late-night online chats helped keep me sane, and I appreciate your insight and comments and, most of all, your friendship. To Amy Johnson Crow, your friendship through thick and thin has been a great support. To Myra Vanderpool Gormley, who I am lucky enough to call my other mother, your love, guidance, support, and jokes bring a smile to my face each day. You saw something in me years ago and helped bring it out. I owe so much to you.

My family, as always, has been there to help me through this latest project. Michael, your willingness to accept my late nights and bizarre schedule is appreciated. Marie, you reminded me to take a moment from time to time to look at the blue sky and enjoy a little fresh air. Ben, your computer knowledge is amazing, and your willingness to explain things to your mother rather than just do them yourself is something I hold dear. Elizabeth and Jessica, your love, hugs, and notes helped keep me going and were no less important to me than the offerings of any one else. I love all of you.

And finally to the many faceless individuals who have e-mailed me over the years and asked me the questions that helped frame this book, may you forge ahead in your research with the latest computer tools at your disposal. Remember to grasp technology.

Icons Used in This Book

 Definitions
Terminology and jargon explained

 Money Saver
Getting the most out of research dollars

 For More Info
Where to turn for more in-depth coverage

 Notes
Thoughts, ideas, and related insights

 Hidden Treasures
Family papers and home sources

 Reminder
"Don't-Forget" items to keep in mind

 Idea Generator
Techniques and prods for further thinking

 Step By Step
Walkthroughs of important procedures

 Important
Information and tips you can't overlook

 Timesaver
Shaving minutes and hours off the clock

 Internet Source
Where on the Web to find what you need

Tip
Ways to make research more efficient

 Library/Archive Source
Repositories that might have the information you need

Warning
Stop before you make a mistake

Table of Contents At a Glance

Table of Contents

Introduction

N owadays, genealogists rely heavily on their computers. Throughout the last few years the computer has managed to insinuate itself into the lives of even the most reluctant of genealogists. After all, many researchers were humming along just fine without the electronic wonder kid, and a few dragged their feet before coming to the conclusion that many of the rest of us had: The computer is a wonderful device to aid us with a wide variety of tasks and issues that we deal with in our research.

Genealogists who are new to the computer remain slightly uncomfortable with it, and as such they haven't yet come to terms with all that it can do. Others have begun to experiment with some of the bells and whistles—the many gadgets that can be used with the computer. Of course, with each new gadget comes a new set of terms that may be totally unfamiliar to the genealogist. After all, genealogists try to spend the bulk of their time using the computer to find more ancestors. Anything that detracts from the time they can set aside for researching their family is often suspect or pushed aside.

With the increased technology now available in regard to scanners, digital cameras, and other equipment, the computer has become much more than a filing system for the genealogist. Researchers can now use their computers to create personalized gifts in which the family tree incorporates so much more than just the dry names, dates, and places. Through the use of a scanner, genealogists can enhance and share their information by digitizing images of original documents. And digital cameras allow researchers to see the shots taken in the family cemetery and know they are accurate images before leaving the area.

These are just a couple of examples of how the computer is now being used. Some of the gadgets that genealogists currently are mastering involve peripherals, such as personal data assistants, or PDAs. Their small size allows a researcher to take their genealogy with them all the time—a great way to compare notes with a potential cousin while on the road or when attending a genealogical conference. Instead of relying on memory when discussing surnames or families, you can whip out your PDA and consult your electronic family tree.

Preservation is another strength of the computer that is too often overlooked. Many people have invested in converting their old 8mm films to videotape. Now those videotapes can be converted to digital files, allowing the researcher to store them on a hard drive, burn them to a CD, and more.

Don't worry if some of this technology is a little hard to comprehend. That's the whole point of this book—to examine the many ways you can use the computer and the latest technologies to record, preserve, and share your family history.

It seems like we have had scanners almost as long as there have been computers. This isn't true, but most of us have acquired a scanner that came with a new computer, or have picked one up as a relatively inexpensive add-on. We are going to see how the scanner is more than just a bargain. We will see how it can do so much more than we originally thought, and how new scanners are offering us features to make it even easier to scan mementos we thought could never be digitized.

Throughout the years, I have spent a lot of time getting to know my computer. I have come to realize that most of what I do in my research is enhanced, sped up, or aided by it. By incorporating my computer into my genealogy, I have forever altered the way I do many things. This is not to say I don't still spend a lot of time using original and primary documents, but the way I arrange my research, and the amount of work I have to do when I get home, has changed. The ways I share the information I have found also have changed. And the methods I use for finding cemeteries, or for getting directions to repositories in cities I haven't visited before, are different now. I owe much of this to my computer and to all the peripherals that are now available.

So let's begin a new journey through the world of computerized family history—more specifically, a look at how you can digitize your family history and the many benefits this can bring you in sharing and preserving your findings.

ONE

What Does it Mean to Digitize Family History?

Idea Generator

Digitizing your family history is the process of creating computerized duplicates of your genealogical information, photos, and documents. Perhaps the best examples of this are the various commercial Web sites, such as Ancestry.com and Genealogy.com, that offer census images that have been scanned and are now available through subscriptions. You also may have access to them through your public library, if your library has subscribed to the ProQuest databases.

The census images we view through these various Web sites offer a digitized copy of the pages that most of us could previously only read on microfilm, through libraries. If we were lucky enough to have a public library with a good genealogy department, then perhaps we were fortunate enough to find the census microfilms there. If not we often had to look elsewhere, such as the Family History Library.

The digitization of censuses is just one example of what is possible with a computer, the correct peripherals, and a little ingenuity. Truly we are no longer limited by a lack of technology. **If we can dream it, most often we can make it happen with our computers.** I continue to marvel at how electronics continually get better, sharper, easier to use, and cheaper.

Of course, when many people think about digitizing, they only think of using a scanner to copy photographs. While that is still one of the most popular ways in which this technology is used, some of you may be brushing off digitizing because it doesn't seem like an option for you. Perhaps all the pictures you are interested in are far from your computer, living at other people's homes. Actually, digitizing your family photos is just one of the many ways in which you can use computers, scanners, and other goodies. Many of the latest crop of scanners offer some wonderful features that give you a freedom you never thought possible. However, digitizing your own pictures is not the only way technology can help you, especially in today's computer market. You may find out that it is much easier to reach those distant cousins—and pictures—than you thought.

A LOOK BACK

Before we go forward, let us take a moment and walk down memory lane— a most appropriate stroll for genealogists, when you think about it.

Too many of us have stories of how the pictures, family Bible, special letters, or other family mementos were given to the one person in the family who refused to share them, at least if it required sending them through the postal system. Let's face it—even with the current abilities to track packages and letters, there are, unfortunately, times when those packages or letters have disappeared. No one wants to be responsible for the family heirlooms going astray. Before tracking numbers and parcel delivery services became more reasonably priced it was even worse. As a result, the family heirlooms all too often remained with a single family member, with others only able to view them if they visited in person.

Sometimes you were lucky—the holder of the family mementos would make photocopies of the Bible pages for you, or perhaps they would write out or type up an abstract of the information found hidden within those precious pages. However, photocopies and transcriptions may go a long way towards preserving the information found in a family Bible, but what about keeping the actual heirloom intact? Until fifteen or twenty years ago, the average person knew little about methods of preserving the various documents in their possession.

Transcriptions, while sometimes the only thing we have to go by, also hold the potential for errors. We are human, after all, and that means we may err, especially when it comes to writing down names or dates. And sometimes a transcription was the only thing we were able to get from the holder of the family heirlooms. It may have been that the cousin didn't have access to a photocopier, or that the Bible was in such a dilapidated state that it could not be duplicated using a traditional copy machine.

No one had personal copiers ten years ago, so many of us would use the photocopier at our place of work. Today that is frowned upon— theft of services—but back then everyone did it and thought nothing of it. Some of the records, however, are fragile, and the constant flipping back and forth of the delicate pages, then flattening them against the copier, may have done more harm than good. If the person realized the damage that might be done, she may have transcribed the information in the book instead. This meant that those of us who received the transcription had to rely on what had been sent and hope that it was an accurate copy. And no matter what, if we were relying on the

Hidden Treasures

PROTECT THOSE DOCUMENTS

Paper lasts a long time, but not forever—if we don't preserve it. You can find out more about how to protect and preserve those fragile, old papers in your files by reading Katherine Scott Sturdevant's *Organizing & Preserving Your Heirloom Documents* (Cincinnati: Betterway Books, 2002).

transcription, our source was always tainted in that it was not the original, and thus forever was open to possible error.

Today's gadgets often allow the individual who is scanning to gather the image without damaging the Bible or letter further by having to feed it through a document feeder, or by flipping it back and forth as each page is copied. As you will see later in the book, there are now a wide variety of ways to scan fragile documents and books. Even our photographs can be fed into scanners that don't damage the originals.

I'D BE HAPPY TO PAY FOR A SET

Before digital cameras and scanners, when it came to photographs that others had, if we wanted our own copies we would offer to pay for a duplicate set to be made from the negatives. Unlike today, back in the 1970s and early 1980s it was unusual to get more than one set of the prints made when you turned the film in for processing. Of course, when offering to pay for a set of prints to be made, we were assuming that the person with the pictures also had the negatives, and that the negatives in question still could be reproduced. I know that in my own personal collection of family photos there are many I do not have negatives of. Of the negatives I do have, there are some that were taken in the 1950s and 1960s that are large and oversized. Getting these reproduced sometimes required finding a photography shop that could handle the special size. This often added to the price of the duplicates.

Of course, offering to pay for a set of prints showed the cousins or family members you were corresponding with that you truly were interested in the pictures they had, and sometimes meant you got a better response from them—perhaps you even got some family stories to go along with the pictures that were sent. But like everything else before the onslaught of computer technology, it took time. For many years one-hour photo shops were simply a pipe dream.

GREAT-GRANDPA'S TOMBSTONE IS UNREADABLE

Today, we frequently take those one-hour photo kiosks for granted when we are getting the film from the family reunion or the trip to the cemetery developed. How many of us drop off our film at the local Wal-Mart while we go about getting other things in the store, and then pick up the pictures at the end of our shopping? We haven't even given a thought to how those pictures would come out until we go back to get them, assuming everything will come out fine.

I suspect, though, that I am not the only one who has had a roll of film develop poorly or even fail to develop at all when it was processed. We are disappointed, maybe even a bit perturbed. Many times we begin to take our

For More Info

CEMETERIES BY FLASHBULB

Genealogists love to spend time in cemeteries. They want a record or proof of their ancestors' final resting place. There are many ways to preserve tombstones through pictures and rubbings. You can find out more in Sharon DeBartolo Carmack's *Your Guide to Cemetery Research* (Cincinnati: Betterway Books, 2002).

Definitions

MEGAPIXELS

One megapixel is equal to 1,048,576 pixels. Megapixel is a term used in graphics display, including your graphics card and cameras. To keep it simple you can think in terms of millions. So a three-megapixel camera creates an image that uses three million pixels, or dots, to create that picture. Usually the higher the number of megapixels the better the image, and the more you can do with it in regard to resizing, or more important, enlarging.

frustration out on the poor unsuspecting clerk. It is bad enough when their equipment somehow messes up my pictures, but I think I am even more frustrated when the bad pictures are my fault, either because of bad lighting or because my arm moved while I was taking the photos.

I am sure that I am not the only one who has felt heartache at the realization that some of the people at the reunion who were in those ruined or unreadable pictures may not be at the next one, or that it will be years before I can go back to that particular cemetery, if ever. Then there is the understanding that my efforts to preserve family history through photographs have been for nothing.

I know people who routinely take three and four shots of each tombstone, in the hopes that at least one of them will come out clear enough that the details can be read. Some make rubbings, though many cemeteries no longer allow this, or take copious notes in an attempt to preserve the stones they may never be able to visit again.

The latest crop of digital cameras offers great alternatives to some of the problems associated with using traditional 35mm cameras. Perhaps the biggest benefit with the digital camera is the ability to preview the picture immediately after taking it. Of course, as we will see later on, there are many more benefits to the digital camera, though it also may mean we need to spend a little time getting familiar with it. You also will see that there is more to picking a digital camera than just looking at the number of megapixels.

YOU'RE STUCK, SO SORRY

All too frequently, before computers, the pictures we took or the photocopies that people sent to us were not the best quality. Unfortunately, this meant that we had to accept the limitations of the photograph or the photocopy and hope that at another time we might have the chance to get a better one. As my family will tell you, though, I seldom accept defeat. I usually look for a better way to do something. It might not always be the easiest way to do it, or the most direct, but if it gives me a better photograph or allows me to read something on a bad photocopy I figure the effort is worth it.

Today's technology makes my previous efforts look truly archaic. The graphics software packages now available allow us to repair and enhance anything that we have digitized, including scanned images and digital photographs. Better still, software prices have been reduced and there are now less expensive, competitive products that offer us real choices about the software we will use to help us with our hobby.

How often have we made a photocopy of a census page at the library, only to be frustrated later by the terrible blackened corners under which our ancestors are hiding? Here we were, trying to be good genealogists by getting copies of the documents on which we find our ancestors, only to be thwarted by the limitations of the technology of the time. Of course, the fact that we could even make a photocopy from the microfilm was a major step forward. Many researchers who began to dabble in the family history hobby in the 1950s and 1960s were limited to transcribing anything they found.

Today, most libraries with microfilmed records provide special photocopiers that read the microfilm and print it to a page for us. While these copiers have been around for years, the latest models offer enhancements that allow us to often eliminate the distortions of some of the hard-to-read sections, bringing names out or at least making them more readable. Even better, some of the more popular genealogical libraries have invested in high-end copiers that also offer a choice of paper size, which can make it easier to organize all of those pages when we get home.

For years we have made photocopies of records and resources we find on microfilm, and we have filed those away in our folder or notebook systems. By digitizing some of those documents, you not only can share them more easily with others, but you have opened a door to publishing a family history that includes wonderful visual aids. We are visual people, and others will appreciate the addition of some of the records you have found. If your research has broken through a brick wall, or the records you digitize help to settle a family feud that has been brewing between researchers for some time, you definitely want to share those records, and digitizing is one of the best ways now available. Later, we will examine the many ways you can scan—not only photographs and papers, but also slides, negatives, and even microfilm.

TAKING IT WITH YOU

One of the biggest advances I see in this wonderful technology is the fact that some of the gadgets have gotten so small. I have seen some personal digital assistants (PDAs) that could break your back when added to a purse that is already carrying everything and the kitchen sink, and ones that I wouldn't advise men put in their pants pocket. However, I have been thrilled to see the newer devices that are coming out, full of power and smaller than ever.

PDAs now offer so much beyond the basics of keeping track of our appointments and phone numbers. And I much prefer to use my PDA to track my genealogy than my dental appointments—genealogy is much more fun. Today's crop of products is embracing a power that makes it possible to carry your family tree with you, thus giving you research opportunities at any time. As you will see later in this book, today's PDAs are almost as good as your desktop, and the genealogical implications are powerful.

You even will see how your PDA can be used to help you find a library in a remote city, or to help identify a tombstone in a cemetery so that you or

For More Info

ORGANIZING ALL THAT PAPER

There are many theories available on how to organize the paper generated by our research of a family tree. One system that prefers all of the records be the same size is William Dollarhide's, which is detailed in *Managing a Genealogical Project* (Baltimore: Genealogical Publishing Company, Inc., 1999).

Reminder

any other researcher can return to it at a later date. You are only held back by your imagination. PDAs no longer just nag us to get to that meeting—instead they can become a true personal assistant to any genealogist.

Not Yet A Paperless Society, But Much More Portable

When personal computers first hit the scene, everyone was crowing about how wonderful computers would be and that we were seeing the beginning of the paperless society. Of course, we now know that isn't quite what happened. The personal computer has cut down on the paper we must have around us in some aspects of genealogy, and has increased it in others (see Figure 1-1 below).

Figure 1-1
Once you have digitized your family photographs, you can bring your family history charts and forms to life.

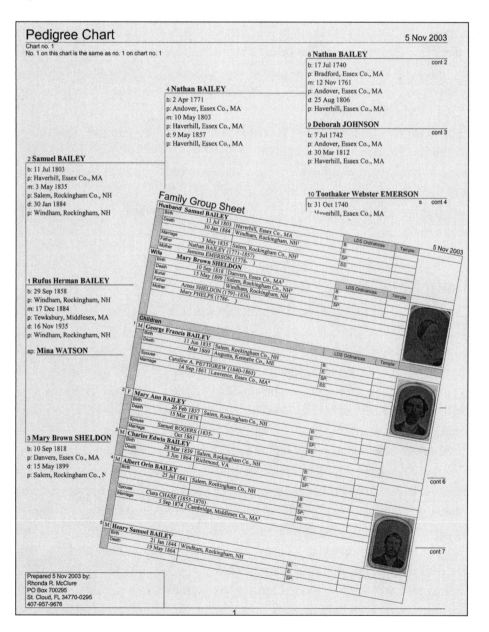

With the computer came the chance to enter information about an ancestor only once and then print that information out in any manner we wanted, including—a family group sheet, pedigree chart, descendant outline, and more. Formatting was all taken care of by the computer, and this freed us up to be able to spend more time researching.

Of course, with the advent of the Internet it seems like we are printing out more than ever before. It is such a changing beast that, all too often, if we don't print out what we find about a particular ancestor when we find it, then we may rue the moment we made the decision not to print. The scenario is too common; upon returning to the site in question the information we wanted about our ancestors has been moved, removed entirely, or changed.

ZIP UP THE WEB

You don't always have to print out everything you find on the Internet. There is a nifty little program that allows you to save the pages of the site in a compressed file, called a Zip file, for use later on. This is a wonderful way to gather information to be used offline later when it is more convenient. *Zip Up the Web* is published by Insight Development and allows you the ability to save not only the text, but also links and graphics for up to five levels of the site. Remember this is just for research, as copyrights still pertain to information found on the Internet. You can find this product at the CreativePro.com Web site, <www.creativepro.com/software/home/882.html>.

So I make it a point to print or somehow save the information I find at the moment I find it. Of course this makes for lots of stacks of paper that have to be filed, but it is a good habit. **We should be saving everything we are basing our research on, including the information found online.** By the same token, as I am zooming around the Internet, I love it when those who are publishing their information include digitized documents such as the family Bible I didn't know existed or other unique records that I may not be able to get to in my lifetime.

Important

Publishing to the Web is not something new, but the way in which some of the family historians are willing to share the documents and photos they have is. By the end of this book, you will find that you can also share your family history in this way if you so choose. You may find that it brings you more contacts via e-mail, rather than less, as some have warned—those who discourage the posting of source citations on the Internet, for instance. Many times when people see documents you've posted online, they will contact you to see what else you may have and to see if they can trade documents with

For More Info

INTERNET PUBLISHING

For an introduction to publishing your family history on the Internet, see my book *The Complete Idiot's Guide to Online Genealogy*, 2d Edition. (Indianapolis: Alpha Books, 2002).

Warning

you so that both of you have a better collection. This has happened to me on a number of instances.

NOT INDEPENDENTLY WEALTHY

Before you can share your documents online or publish them in print, you must first learn about the many opportunities now available. In the past, most genealogists were deterred from publishing their family histories by the high cost. We dearly wanted to, but when we began to investigate the costs involved in going through a vanity press—the only real option for most genealogists—the sticker shock was often enough to cancel any plans for publishing.

Today's publishing technology—the high-quality, low-cost options found in today's printers, for example—is just one of the ways computers make publishing easier and cheaper for genealogists. Of course, the Internet also offers a place to publish your work in progress, reaching cousins who will dialogue with you and perhaps offer details or corrections so that when you do finally publish a book, it is the best it can be.

But like so many aspects of genealogy and computers, there is a learning curve here. Too often as you go into the computer store or begin to investigate possible peripherals, you find yourself intimidated by all the computer terms and abbreviations. This is more true in the genealogical community—so many family historians grew up without computers and have been dragged into the medium by their children or grandchildren, who can't seem to go but a few minutes without a technology fix.

The good news is that you probably have an expert in the family who you can turn to when you are confused about what is out there. Unfortunately, it has been my experience that genealogists think differently from the geeks who create the gadgets and gizmos. We often must take what is there and manipulate it to our own interest. There are some wonderful contraptions out there that, when they were invented, were never conceived for genealogical purposes, but that when used correctly can aid us greatly.

Quite frankly, I think this is the case with most things genealogists use in all aspects of their search for family history. If you think about it, even the records that we rely on so heavily were created for completely nongenealogical reasons, and yet genealogists have found ways to make them work in their hobby. Of course, just as you find limitations and frustrations with records, there are sometimes similar problems with electronic peripherals— though the biggest problem with the computer toys is the communication gap. Genealogists know what they want, but sometimes they can't put it into "geek speak" so that the salesman at the computer store understands what the genealogist is trying to do.

You may be thinking that you will never be able to grasp the "geek speak," but I know better. Recently my husband asked me what I wanted for my birthday. In the past I would have had some vague response about "wishing I could identify tombstones using a GPS system." This time, however, I had done my homework, and when I told him what I wanted, it included the make and model. I even included the part number. This made an impression on him—he commented on it later when we had dinner with a "geek" colleague of his.

The goal of this book is not only to introduce you to all the different ways you can digitize your family history, but also to get you comfortable with the important features to look for when investigating necessary hardware options. This way you are an informed consumer and will not rely solely on the "sale of the century" that the salesman is pushing for that week. You will know what types of products exist and how the specifications affect the projects you have in mind—not to mention the whole reason you are purchasing this add-on in the first place. Just as I have begun to research the peripherals and make sense of the technical specifications, you will soon find that it no longer seems as unintelligible as it once was.

In the end you should come away with some great ideas for how you can not only digitize, but also preserve and share, your family history. Computers are not as scary or intimidating as we sometimes think. When you know how to walk the walk and talk the talk, you will find that it is like anything else you work with in genealogy—just a matter of course.

With that said, let's get started. Scanners are perhaps the most popular peripheral when it comes to computers, and not just for genealogists. In fact, scanners are probably the first peripheral that many computer users invest in.

TWO

An Introduction to the Scanner

A scanner can be different things to different people. To some it is a way to convert many laboriously typed pages of a personal family history manuscript into a word processing document. To others it is a way to copy family photos or the pages of the family Bible to share with cousins near and far, without subjecting the original photos or Bible to further wear and tear. To still others, the scanner offers an inexpensive way to enhance a soon-to-be-published family history with wonderful graphics of documents or previously unavailable photographs.

Regardless of what you think a scanner is and why you might be considering getting one (or learning how to use the one that came with the computer system you bought last year), a scanner is an extension of your computer. **It is designed to take an object—usually a photograph or piece of paper—and reproduce an identical digital image that the computer can then use in any number of ways, including displaying it or adding it to a multitude of programs.**

\di'fin\ *vb*

Definitions

SCANNER 101

Because scanners are an extension of the computer, it should not surprise us that the descriptions on the sides of scanner boxes sometimes feel like they are in some as of yet unknown language—no doubt shared with a select few by the same aliens who dropped some of our ancestors off around the globe, to add to our frustration. You may even be scratching your head as you read the product information and mentally kicking yourself, because you realize that you still don't understand enough "techie" to decide if the scanner in question will do what you need it to or if you should get a more expensive one.

Before you can decide what scanner would be the best for you, it is important to recognize the different types of scanners that exist. Each one has its strengths and weaknesses. Some may be beneficial when traveling, while others may need to simply sit on the desk in your office, waiting for you to return with photocopied records to digitize.

Scanners of All Shapes and Sizes

I suspect that when you hear the term *scanner*, one of two types comes immediately to mind. The first is the *flatbed* variety; the other is the *sheetfed* type. Most people have the flatbed variety because it works well with just about anything you are trying to scan, provided the item fits nicely on the glass plate. Oversized books, depending on where you have placed the scanner in your office, may prove tricky as you try to capture as much of the page as possible without shifting the book while the machine is performing the scan.

The flatbed scanner sits on a table or other flat surface, and as the name implies, it has a flat glass surface onto which you lay the original, usually facedown (see Figure 2-1 below). Like a photocopier, the scanner's mechanism moves across the original from under the glass plate. The image is then displayed on your computer's monitor. Most flatbed scanners can handle up to an $8\frac{1}{2}'' \times 14''$ page at the most.

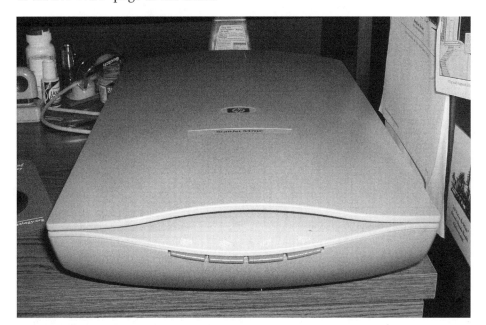

Figure 2-1
Flatbed scanners are easy to use, but do require a lot of desk space.

Of course, even if the flatbed scanner can handle only a $8\frac{1}{2}'' \times 11''$ page, you have to figure that the dimensions of the scanner itself will be bigger than the size of the page. Most of them are at least an inch all around, meaning you have to have desk, table, or flat surface space for a gadget that is at least $11'' \times 13'' \times 3''$, though I should point out that many of the latest flatbed scanners are much thinner. For some of us, our desk is some of the most prime real estate in the city. And because the scanner is a flat surface, it sometimes finds itself doubling as a place to put files and other things.

IT'S NOT A PART OF YOUR DESK

Genealogists never have enough desk space. We are forever building piles as we work from one file to the next. Even those of us who are relatively organized have our moments when we have piles around us. And having a flatbed scanner on the desk does not ensure that the scanner is always accessible.

Too often we treat it like a part of the desk, piling things on top of it. Be careful when you do this. Remember that it has a large piece of glass and that the bulk of it is made of plastic. Ideally you shouldn't put anything on top of the scanner, but let's face it, we are not living in an ideal world.

You definitely do not want to have anything sitting on top of the scanner when you are using it, other than perhaps the next piece of paper or photograph you need to scan.

The better care you take of your scanner, the better images it will deliver to you.

Because this type of scanner often requires you to turn the photo or page facedown, the potential for the scanned image to be slightly askew increases. While most people put the document or photo up against the upper right corner to try to straighten it out, there are times when I have been scanning a page from a book and the resulting image was slanted a bit. When I discovered this during the preview pass of the scanner, I often would debate whether or not another preview pass needed to be done after repositioning the book.

The *sheetfed* scanner is usually a more compact machine (see Figure 2-2 on page 15). Because the mechanisms in the sheetfed scanner move the sheet along instead of moving the scanning head or light, it can be much smaller. The potential for a slightly tilted scan is still a possibility, as the rollers that grab the page and send it under the scanner head may not grab the page evenly, or you may not have put the page into the scanner correctly.

With the sheetfed scanner, as the name implies, you are feeding a single page through the scanner at a time. Some say this gives a better scan, and assuming the rollers have grabbed the page accordingly, it should scan straight. Of course, I am sure that you can see one of the biggest drawbacks to this type of scanner. Each page you wish to scan must be a single sheet. This means that if the page in question is bound in a book, then it is not possible to use this type of scanner to make a copy.

Reminder

JUST LIKE THE OLD DAYS

If you have ever used a fax machine, you have used a sheetfed scanner of sorts—that is how the fax machine sends your pages via the phone lines. It feeds the pages one at a time over the scanner head, and the fax's brain then converts the data to something that can be sent through the line, where the receiving fax converts the data and prints it out.

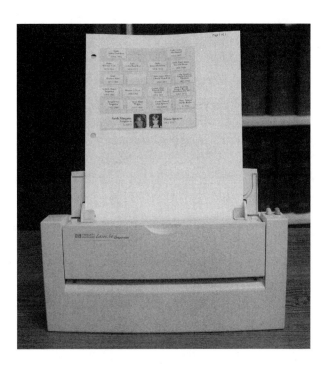

Figure 2-2
Sheetfed scanners can only be used when scanning single sheets, and should never be used on any delicate documents or photos.

Timesaver

One of the benefits of the sheetfed scanner is that, like a copier, you often can set it to scan multiple pages without your having to manually begin each scan. For instance, if you had a printed family story on five or six pages and you didn't want to baby-sit the scanner, telling the computer when to scan each page, the sheetfed scanner could be an option. Of course, like the photocopier, it is possible that a page will be grabbed off-kilter or two pages will be pulled through at the same time, so you will want to make sure that you look closely at the resulting images or pages on your computer.

A third type of scanner is the *handheld* scanner, which now comes in many different styles. Originally the handheld scanner's head was about 4″ wide. Unlike the flatbed or sheetfed designs, the motor—the method for moving the scanner head—is completely human-driven. Handheld scanners piqued the interest of some forward-thinking genealogists a few years back because they hoped to take them on the road, attached to their notebook computers, scanning all manner of things as they went from cousin to cousin or courthouse to library.

Of course the reality is sometimes far from the dream, and this was never truer than with the original handheld scanners. Because the scan was dependent on the smoothness of the motion of your hand as you dragged it across the picture or page, the resulting image sometimes had a noticeable break in it, even when you were sure you hadn't stopped for a microsecond when dragging the scanner. As such, more often than not it would take more than a single pass per photograph or document to get a reasonable scan. While handheld scanners are definitely small enough to take on the road, few genealogists have jumped on this bandwagon because of the frustrations in getting a good scan.

Today, I see more about *pen* scanners than I do about the wider, more traditional handheld scanners. The pen scanner is capable of scanning a single line of text at a time. Let me stress that when I mean text, I mean the printed word. Generally the records genealogists view in various courthouse deed and probate books use letters too tall for the pen scanner to handle. However, pen scanners are excellent tools for scanning small biographies, for instance, rather than having to transcribe them by hand. The pen scanner can handle text from an eight point to a twenty point font. Another benefit of the pen scanner is that you do not have to manipulate the book in any way to make it lay flat, thus protecting the spine of the volume from any additional damage. The pen scanner, unlike the other scanners discussed here, is limited to the scanning of text, which it then converts using optical character recognition (OCR) to create a file that is recognized by your computer, usually your word processing program.

UNDERSTANDING OCR

Optical Character Recognition (OCR) is how the computer converts a scanned image of text on a page to text in a word processing file. OCR software is designed to look at each of the letters, identifying each one based on its darkened form. And that is what sometimes causes a problem. Older, typeset books sometimes have marks of ink that the OCR software thinks should be part of the letter it is trying to read. As a result, the digitized copy sometimes contains some strange, incorrect words.

Today's crop of OCR programs is more sensitive and often recognizes quirks in the printed page that should be ignored. However, no program is infallible. If you run things through an OCR program, proofread the digitized copy carefully while you still have access to the original document you converted.

One scanner that has become more popular is the *photo* scanner (see Figure 2-3 on page 17). You have no doubt guessed, based on the name, that this scanner is designed to digitize photos. Many photo scanners resemble other flatbed scanners and may be capable of scanning photographs up to $8'' \times 11''$ in size. Others are much smaller, designed to handle the $4'' \times 5''$ photos that so many of us have piled up over the years. In fact, many of the newer flatbed scanners are labeled as photo scanners, which means you get the benefits of a flatbed scanner along with features designed to making scanning photos easier. Sometimes photo scanners come with different bundled software packages designed specifically for enhancing or working with photographs as well.

The photo scanners that are designed to work with just the $4'' \times 6''$ prints sometimes have a drawer that opens. You place the picture in question into the drawer, where it is retracted into the scanner during the scanning process. These drawers are designed to protect the photograph, so this method may be one to consider for some of your more fragile photographs.

Photo scanners are sometimes combined with a *negative* or *film* scanner. These scanners are usually the smaller ones. Their focus is on digitizing negative strips, usually of the 35mm variety. I don't know of any that talk about scanning the old 110 camera negatives, and some of them require a special attachment to handle the newer 24mm negatives that come with Advanced Photo System (APS) prints.

Negative scanners, or photo scanners that support the scanning of negatives, require additional light. As we will discuss in more detail later in this chapter, and as you have noticed if you have scanned anything or used a photocopier, there is a light that moves along the image you have placed on the glass of your standard scanner. This is what reads the image, and it works because the back of the image is solid. When using a negative scanner, the negative must be illuminated from behind for the scanner to identify the image—much like we must hold a negative or slide up to a light to see it with our naked eye.

Notes

ADVANCED PHOTO SYSTEM

Advanced Photo System cameras allow you to take normal pictures as well as panoramic views, photos that are much wider than a standard photograph. Kodak's Advantix cameras are an example of this system. By making certain selections on the camera before taking the picture, you can get a print size of 3″ × 5″ or 4″ × 6″ (classic), 3″ × 6″ or 4″ × 7″ (high-definition television, or HDTV), or 3″ × 10″ or 4″ × 11″ (panoramic).

Figure 2-3
Photo scanners may help preserve the colors of the photograph and are often smaller versions of flat bed scanners.

If you want to get the best of both worlds, then you will want to look for a flatbed photo scanner that offers a transparency adapter (see Figure 2-4 on page 18). A transparency adapter is a light source that can be hooked into the scanner and placed over the negative strip or slides, which are placed facedown on the glass of the scanner, usually in a specially designed holder that blocks out

Tip

light except as it comes through the negative or slide. As the scanner begins its pass, the transparency adapter lights up the negative.

Scanners that include transparency adapters can recognize when the image that has been scanned is a negative or a slide. They automatically adjust the resulting digitized image accordingly, allowing for the appropriate colors. This differs from the standard scan, which is more of an exact replica of the original document or photo. If the scanner were to make an exact replica of the negative strip, we would need to do a lot of work on the image once it was on the computer. We would have to manually reverse the image from negative to positive, and it is possible that we might also have to spend considerable time colorizing and enhancing it as well.

High-end negative scanners are another breed. They can scan only negative strips or individual slides. They often have a higher quality in dots per inch (DPI) to the final scan, and also usually have a corresponding higher price tag. They were not designed for genealogists on a budget, but for photographers who were digitizing all of their material and wanted the best possible digital images. While these specialized products no longer cost thousands of dollars, they do tend to hover around five hundred dollars.

If all of your photographs are on slides—and I grew up around many people who routinely had their film developed to slides—this type of film scanner might be a worthwhile investment, as it is truly the best at getting good scans from negatives or slides.

OPEN UP AND SAY "AH"

While we have talked about the different types of scanners, I thought we should take a moment and discuss just what happens when the scanner makes

Figure 2-4
Transparency adapters offer a backlight so that the scanner can view negatives and slides.

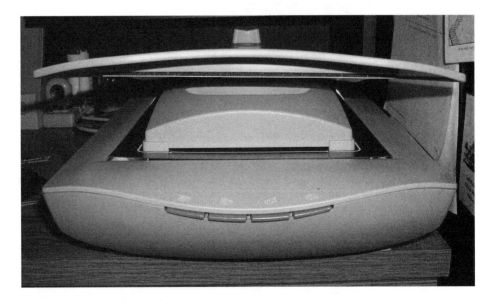

DPI VS. SPI

DPI, or "dots per inch," is a way of identifying the resolution of a printer. The theory is that the more dots per inch, the smoother and less grainy the printed picture. Scanners should be measured in SPI—samples per inch—which refers to the individual sensors on the scanner head. However, since SPI and DPI are the same measurement, you will find that the resolution of most scanners is listed in dots per inch and that most magazines, books, and Web sites discussing scanner resolution will list it as DPI.

a pass over the photograph or document. In doing so, you also will be introduced to some of the parts of your scanner so, hopefully, it won't seem as foreign to you when we get done.

The most important part of your scanner is the sensor, or the scanner *head*. This is the eye of your scanner, and it works much like your own eyes do. As the scanner head moves along the picture or document, the sensor, which is made up of many individual photosensitive cells, records the amount of light that bounces back as the scanner head's light passes over the original document. The darker the surface of the original, the less current is received by those photosensitive cells; the lighter or brighter the original, the more received current. Just like you, your scanner has a brain. The scanner's brain is designed to receive and translate the electrical current sent by the photosensitive cells, just as your brain receives the impulses from your own eyes.

Important

We already mentioned DPI earlier, but here is where you begin to understand what that number means. Each photosensitive cell on the sensor is designed to read a single dot of the original image. So if the scanner in question claims to scan at 2,400 DPI, that means there are 2,400 photosensitive cells per inch reproducing the original. Generally speaking, the higher the number, the more clear your digitized copy.

The scanner head needs something besides the photosensitive cells to do its job. It also needs a light to reflect onto the original document. Remember, it is this reflected light that those cells are registering and sending to the scanner's brain. And let's not forget that your scanner does have a brain. It is not nearly as intricate as the central processing unit (CPU) running your computer, or as the brain that helps you get up and tie your shoes in the morning, but without it the scanner would just be a lovely, rather expensive paperweight.

Most of today's scanners require two more things to be effective. The first is power, and that usually requires that the scanner be near a wall outlet, as most of their power cables only reach about five feet or so. The other important cable that hangs off the back of your scanner is the interface cable, which does exactly that: allows your scanner to interface—or talk—with your computer.

LET'S INTERFACE

The interface is another way in which the geeks like to get us. There are many different types of interface methods, and you will find that each has its staunch supporters. In fact, in geek circles, discussions of methods of interface bring about the same passion as discussions about the best genealogy programs do among computer genealogists. And in both cases, there is perhaps no right answer other than the one that works for you.

Reminder

The most popular types of interface for scanners include:

- *Parallel port* (also known as a printer port) can be found on any computer, and for those running older computers may be the only option available to connect a scanner to the computer. The downside to a scanner that interfaces with the computer through a parallel port is the speed of transfer. It is very slow, and given that scanned images are often extremely large files, you may not have the patience needed.

- *USB port* (universal serial bus) has become the standard over the last couple of years. In fact, version 2.0 of USB has taken what was already a relatively fast method of transfer and increased it. If you are using a computer built in the last few years you are sure to have at least one USB port, and it's more than likely you have two or more. One of the benefits of scanners that connect via USB is that, generally speaking, the operating system (Windows or Mac) is designed to recognize the new item plugged in with little work on your part.

- *FireWire* (IEEE-1394 High Performance Serial Bus) is the next fastest method. This is, as the name implies, a speedy method of transferring data from the scanner to the computer. The downside to this method is that fewer computers have a FireWire connector, though like the USB it is available and supported by both Windows and Mac systems. Another downside to the FireWire is that scanners that support this interface are often more costly, and there are fewer to choose from.

- *SCSI* (pronounced "skuzzy," stands for Small Computer Systems Interface) has been around for a long time. I was introduced to the SCSI interface when my husband purchased our first scanner. The SCSI interface, while fast, is higher up on the learning curve—it requires that you install an actual piece of equipment into the innards of your desktop computer.

In addition to some of the pros and cons I have mentioned in each of the different types of interface, the biggest consideration for what type of a scanner you may be able to get will depend largely on the capabilities of your computer. For instance, if your computer doesn't offer a FireWire port already and you buy a scanner that uses FireWire, then you will find that you either must return that scanner and choose a different one or go out and purchase a FireWire adapter card. While not a truly expensive purchase, it may add up if you have to hire someone to put it in for you. The adapter card is a computer board that fits inside your desktop computer and connects to the motherboard.

For those looking to use FireWire on their notebook computer, it is a little easier. The adapter simply slides into the existing PCMCIA slot where you may put a modem card. The PCMCIA adapter card is slightly larger and thicker than a business card.

GOTTA HAVE THE ADD-ONS—OR DO YOU?

It used to be, when you bought a computer, everything but the printer came with it. Over the years we have seen a big change where that is concerned, primarily because of all of the add-ons available to allow you to do more with your computer. The same can be said about scanners. In the past, you got what you got, and you learned to work around any limitations. Today there are many different types of scanners, as you have seen, along with a variety of add-ons that can take the scanner you have and make it better.

By far the flatbed scanner is the most versatile and the easiest to use. However, if you have many pages or photographs to scan you may quickly reach your limit of "fun" as you lift up the cover of the scanner, position the document or photo, close the cover, either push the scan button on the scanner or tell the scanner software to scan, save the scanned image, and then repeat all these steps again for the next photo or document.

Sheet Feeder to the Rescue

Again, the best of both worlds may be an option here. If you like the versatility of the flatbed scanner, but you also want to do a few projects that are docu-

Definitions

MOTHERBOARD CONTROLS THE COMPUTER

Like a mother is often the backbone of a family, the motherboard is the backbone of the computer. All the other components of the computer meet at the motherboard. If the motherboard isn't working right, the computer has problems, just like a house sometimes begins to fall apart when the mother is sick or away.

Reminder

PCMCIA CARD—NO, NOT ALPHABET SOUP

PCMCIA is the acronym for Personal Computer Memory Card International Association. (Now you can see why it is always listed as its acronym.) The trade association for which the card is named was founded in 1989, and it established standards for the PCMCIA Card, or PC Card—a credit card-sized card that, when plugged in, allows your notebook computer to use peripherals such as modems, networking adapters, CD-ROMs, and other external drives.

ment or photo intensive, you may want to investigate those flatbed scanners that either come with or offer an optional sheet feed adapter. This way you have the flexibility to scan almost anything on the flatbed portion, but when working with multiple pages, you can put them in the sheet feeder and let it go. Most sheet feeder adapters handle multiple pages, and you can set it to scan the documents and save them while you are working on something else or not even sitting at the computer.

THE LIGHTING IS ALL WRONG

I have already mentioned transparency adapters, which convert your flatbed scanner into a negative scanner. The scanned images may not be as sharp as those you would get if you invested in a film scanner, but given the costs of film scanners, this may be an acceptable trade-off. However, as we will see in chapter four, there may be ways to work around scanner limitations once you have the image on your computer and open in your graphics software.

Transparency adapters come in many different shapes and sizes. I prefer those that allow me to set up at least four slides or a full negative strip. While I still must scan them individually, I can set up a group of pictures and then run all four scans before I have to do any additional set up.

Usually flatbed scanners that offer a transparency adapter will supply you

SHEET-FEED THOSE PHOTOS?

One of the newest sheet-fed adapters to come out is one that will feed your 3″×5″ or 4″×6″ photos into the scanner so that you don't have to sit there and manually feed each one. I recently was investigating scanners at a computer show and was intrigued with the HP Scanjet 5500. This flatbed scanner has a sheet-feed adapter on it specifically designed for photos. As I watched it pull the photographs through I began to get concerned that the photos might get damaged as they were dragged across the plate glass of the flatbed, so I asked the product representatives if they had considered that.

It turns out that indeed they had. This particular model, with the automatic photo feeder (APF), uses an interesting approach to protect the photos. An air vacuum belt moves the photos along so they are not actually touching the glass while they are moving—only when they are being scanned. This protects both them and the glass from any possible scratches.

If you find a photo scanner that you are interested in and it has a sheet feed, you may want to research how it feeds the photos through. While you want to digitize the photos, you don't want them to get ruined in the process.

with one or more specially designed sheets into which you can slide or place the filmstrip or individual slides. They are usually black and are designed to block out all of the transparency light except where it shows through the slide or negative. Otherwise, as the scanner head's light goes by, the transparency adapter's light will confuse the scanner, resulting in a very strange scan showing bright patches where the transparency adapter's light managed to get through.

ONE-BUTTON SCANNING

Another feature of many of the latest scanners, especially the flatbeds, is the inclusion of buttons on the front panel. My current flatbed scanner offers buttons to scan, print, e-mail, and fax. Others I have seen offer one-button options that act like a copy machine, and some even offer a "file" option.

One-button scanning saves you from having to go through a number of steps. As we discussed earlier, after you have placed the original on the scanner, you must open the scanner software on your computer and then click the appropriate toolbar button or menu item to start the scan. With one-button scanning, you press the button on the scanner and it launches the program and starts the scan. This is a great feature to have when sending photos directly to the printer or using the scanner as a copy machine. Even if you are planning to publish the scanned photograph or document in your family history, the initial scanning may not need your careful attention, as it is likely you will be editing that image, as will be discussed in chapter eight, once it has been digitized.

Timesaver

KNOW BEFORE YOU GO

While you are now more familiar with the different types of scanners and forms of interfacing them with your computer, I still think it is a good idea to research any product, especially computer products, before you get to the store. Too often I see salesmen pitching a product because that is the product they have been told to pitch for the week. It is all in the marketing, and just because the scanner company's marketing department is tops does not necessarily mean the scanner itself is.

There are a number of places you can go to get more information about scanners. I have included a list of the various companies that design and sell scanners, as you will often get a great deal of technical background information at these sites. I also listed sites where I have found useful, informative, and easy to read reviews of the different scanners, especially the hot-off-the-presses brand new ones.

The list of companies that manufacture scanners on page 24 is limited to those that are the most popular, offer a wide variety of scanners, or offer specialty scanners at the least expensive prices I could find.

SCANNER MANUFACTURERS				
Company	Contact Information	Web Site	Types of Scanners	General Pricing
Antec	(888) 542-6832	<www.antec-inc.com>	Portable sheetfed scanner	Under $50
Canon	(800) 652-2666	<www.usa.canon.com>	Flatbed, sheetfed, photo, film	Under $50 to $1,000
Epson	(800) 873-7766	<www.epson.com>	Flatbed, photo	$150 to $2,500
Hewlett-Packard (HP)	(800) 752-0900	<www.hp.com>	Flatbed, sheetfed, photo, film	Under $70 to $900
Konica Minolta	Contact is via form on their Web site	<www.konicaminolta.us>	Film	$280 to $3,200
Microtek	(310) 687-5940	<www.microtekusa.com>	Flatbed	Under $70 to $375
Nikon	(800) NIKON-UX	<www.nikonusa.com>	Film	$800 to $2,500
SmartDisk	(239) 425-4080 (or via form on their Web site)	<www.smartdisk.com>	Film	$220 to $450
WizCom	(888) 777-0552	<www.wizcomtech.com>	Pen	$125 to $230

WHERE TO GO FOR GUIDANCE

Reminder

I already have suggested that you find your guidance about scanners somewhere other than the salesman at the computer store. This is not meant to disparage the salesman, but it has been my experience in recent years that salesmen often are prompted to push certain products and, given the fact that I am spending my hard-earned money, I like to believe I am getting the best possible product for my goals and my dollars. This often requires me to do some sleuthing—not only to find the specifications I need about the products I have in mind, but more important, to see if I can find individuals who have used them and see what their comments are about them.

Manufacturers' Web sites now go a long way to supply valuable technical information about their individual products. In some instances I have found complete manuals, which I find offer great insight into the intricacies of the product. After all, if the manual is too involved, then I may not have the patience needed to master the new device. I am a genealogist first and a computer geek second, and that means I have no patience whatsoever—and I never bother to read the computer screen or the help files.

Of course, while the manufacturers' Web sites supply technical data as to the specifications of their products, they seldom point out any negatives, giving only glowing remarks about all a consumer can do with it. I prefer to find bulletin boards or reviews from computer magazines and Web sites that offer more honest opinions of the products in question. And, if I can get the chance to see the product in action, all the better.

Some of the sites mentioned below may require a subscription to get the most out of their reviews, as many of them are links to various computer periodicals. However, I find the information in them invaluable when deciding on new hardware or software.

- Flatbed Scanner Review <www.flatbed-scanner-review.org>
- *Macworld* <www.macworld.com>
- *PC Magazine* <www.pcmag.com>
- *SmartComputing* <www.smartcomputing.com>
- ZDNet Reviews <http://reviews-zdnet.com.com/?legacy=cnet>

ON TO THE GOOD STUFF

By now you have a good overview of different types of scanners, and you may be leaning toward a particular one. Now it is on to the fun: the scanning of your photographs and papers. It is best to begin with these before working with negatives and slides so that you are familiar with the scanner and can compare the scanned image to your original picture (something that is almost impossible to do with negatives and slides) to make sure you are using the scanner correctly.

THREE

Scanning Your Photos and Papers

I still remember the first scanner my husband and I got. They weren't scanning in color at the time, just black and white. It was a flatbed scanner, and it was a heavy beast that took up quite a bit of space on the desk. However, we used that scanner a lot, primarily because of the novelty. After all, scanners were a new peripheral at the time—this was almost fourteen years ago. My husband didn't seem to mind the time it took to scan something, whereas I was often quite impatient. Of course, perhaps that has something to do with the fact that I am a genealogist and want it all right now, and he just likes to play with computers.

But scanning back then was extremely slow, which is not surprising when you consider that the computers back then were equally slow when compared to the lightning speeds of today's models. I marvel that we got anything accomplished then with the technology available, given our computer's speed issues and many user-unfriendly aspects.

About four years after we got that scanner I was introduced to what would become my next scanner, this one in color. I was involved in a magazine article in which a family was introduced to a genealogy program and shown how to use it. One of the reasons the family wanted to use the genealogy program selected, which is no longer available, was because of its ability to handle photographs. In addition to bringing me in to show the family how to use the genealogy software, someone was brought in from a computer company with one of its latest scanners. It was an interesting day—the guy from the scanner company was in awe of the genealogy software I was showing, and I was in awe of his scanner. Having some knowledge of scanners, I asked some questions to get an idea of what it could do. And then I asked the big question: Just how much did it cost?

When the price he quoted me didn't send me into heart failure, I decided that when I got home, I would begin to work on my husband about upgrading my scanner to this new one. It would take me another six months or so, but I would eventually get the color scanner, and what a dream that was.

Like the earlier one, it was a flatbed, so it took up as much, if not a little more, room on my desk. While it was supposed to be faster, I wasn't scanning photographs in nanoseconds. But the images were a higher quality, and I could now scan my many color photographs in color, which was a bonus.

Through the years I have learned a few things about scanning, and my husband and I have had discussions about image resolutions. His thinking is the lower the resolution the better. I have long disagreed with that premise; I'm willing to sacrifice disk space for a better image, especially if I want to print that image out.

My issue with the resolution is my need for perfection, something that in the past often had to be sacrificed when it came to facing the limitations of technology. Today's scanners, even the cheapest—those less than a hundred dollars—have a higher resolution than that scanner I paid much more for about ten years ago. That could explain why it wasn't until recently that I began to truly embrace the area of scanning as it applies to genealogy.

TOO MANY DOTS

My main problem with the images I could scan had to do with the "dots" I could see on the image after I printed it (see Figure 3-1 on page 28). This was actually not all my scanner's fault, as printers also have come a long way in the past few years. The printed image looked pixilated—the official term for those dots I was seeing—and to me the poor quality wasn't worth the effort and cost of scanning and printing at that time.

Definitions

RESOLUTION

Resolution is used in many different ways in the computer world. When it comes to the resolution at which a photo is scanned, the lower the number, the less clear the resulting digital image will be, as there are fewer dots of color per inch. The higher the resolution, the more dots per inch and the clearer the picture looks.

PRECIOUS HEIRLOOM PAGES

Some of us are lucky enough to have original land deeds or a marriage license handed down from a great-grandmother that she protected throughout her life. Original, older documents that we may be fortunate enough to have in our possession need to be treated with kid gloves. The less we do with them, the longer they will survive. When scanning any document, take some time to really look at it before you run it through a scanner. Take notice of any fraying of the ends, or if it has been folded, see if the creases are beginning to wear. Any signs of tearing also should be noted. If a document shows any of these or any other signs of fragility, a flatbed scanner is the only safe way to digitize it.

Figure 3-1
Grainy pictures were often a problem with earlier digital cameras and printers.

The technology behind today's scanners and printers has rendered this issue a moot point. I can digitize high-quality images, and I think that by scanning precious documents and working with the scanned images when sharing with family members, I am helping to preserve the originals. Now my originals can be put up to protect them from the elements and from unnecessary handling. In fact, the scanned images are so clear and duplicate the color of the originals so well, I don't feel I am missing anything by not handling the originals.

In the last chapter you were introduced to the many different types of scanners. While I have used many of them, when it comes to my heirloom or older photographs and documents I much prefer the flatbed scanners. I feel they are easier on these more fragile documents.

For most of the things I end up scanning, **I find that the flatbed offers everything I need while giving me control of the original in such a way that I am not worried about harming it.** I have scanned a wide range of photographs, from tintypes to the latest prints I had made at the local one-hour photo shop. However, I also find that I can take advantage of scanning information from newspapers, books, or oversized items with relative ease.

Important

WHAT CAN YOU SCAN?

I already have mentioned some of the things you can scan, though each depends on the type of scanner you decide to purchase. Even if you had your heart set on a particular type of scanner, you may find that, after we have discussed some of the issues with scanning photos and documents, your original choice is no longer the best possible scanner for what you will be doing. Remember to keep an open mind and to do your homework on any scanner before you purchase one.

If you already have a scanner, you may be limited as to what you can scan because of the limitations of that equipment. But perhaps as you are reading through this chapter you will find ideas for the next time you decide to purchase a new one.

WHAT CAN I SCAN?

Anything. You are limited only by your own creativity. While documents and photographs immediately come to mind, here are some other things you may have that you may want to digitize, and a scanner might be one way to do that:

- Picture frames

- Calling cards

- Needlework

- Any cloth or piece of material

- License plates

- Diaries

- Dog tags

Basically, if you can get part or all of the item to lay flat, and if you have a flatbed scanner, you can scan anything. Other types of scanners are not as flexible, since most control the maximum size of the items with a drawer that opens up or with the width of the rollers that feed items through the scanner.

Depending on the type of scanner you already have or have elected to purchase, you may have the potential to scan anything. This means thinking beyond photographs, though of course those may be some of the most important things in regard to your family history. However, if you have old documents, such as family letters, diaries, land records, or mementos, you may want to scan those as well, especially if you want to share them with other family members. If you send them printed versions of digitized items and they don't make it—getting lost in the mail—you will not be devastated by the fact that an irreplaceable family heirloom has been lost. Instead you would simply print another one to send at the expense of only a few extra dollars.

WORKING WITH PHOTOGRAPHS

If you have scanned only a couple of photographs you may not have been happy with the outcome. This may be more a result of a lack of understanding of the proper settings for your scanner or the types of software that can help you enhance the image than with the technology itself, especially if you recently got the scanner. With the correct settings and software, shadows and smudges can be reduced and scratches and other imperfections can be eliminated—or at least rendered less noticeable.

Scanning anything well does require a little patience and sometimes some creative thinking. Remember that the scanner's job is primarily to make a digitized image that your computer can recognize and work with. Enhancements and other special effects are better done through graphics software, which has been specifically designed to work with these images.

Reminder

PROTECTING THE ORIGINAL

Just as you are digitizing records or heirlooms so as not to cause further damage to the originals, you may want to consider storing your original scans as well, working from a copy of each file.

This was the suggestion of an attendee at a seminar I recently gave in which scanners were discussed. It is a good suggestion. If you should make a mistake, or worse yet you make a mistake and then click the "save" button only to discover a mistake or the fact that you don't like the way it prints, you may need to rescan the item.

Instead of working with original images, try using your CD-ROM to copy your originals on CDs. At the very least, save them in another directory on your hard drive so that, should you make a mistake and need to start over, you still have the originals.

There are many great software packages mentioned in chapter eight, where we discuss how to get the most out of your digitized image. You will find that you need not spend an arm and a leg on a package to get one that will do great things.

First, of course, you need to scan the photograph or document, and this requires a little understanding of your scanner. You need to understand how changing the settings will affect the image the computer eventually will work with.

Most of today's scanners have a relatively high resolution, allowing you some flexibility when it comes to being able to enlarge the image or make any major changes. And if the original document or photo is in pristine condition, it may not be necessary to work in graphics software at all, so again the settings for saving the file may need to be altered if you are thinking about sending the image to the Web or are planning to print it.

Scanners come with a default resolution, and this varies by make and model. You may find information about the default discussed in the documentation that comes with the scanner. Of course, since we seldom read the manuals or other documentation that comes with any software or hardware we use, don't worry if you don't know this magic number already. Most of the time it will not be necessary to change the default, but understanding what the higher or lower resolutions will do to the digitized image may save you some headaches later on.

Resolution	What is it Good For?	Color Depth
72 dpi	Publishing any graphics, including line art, to the Web	8-bit (line art); 24-bit for other things
150 dpi	Scanning halftones (such as original newspapers)	24-bit
200 dpi	Line art that is sent to the printer	8-bit
300 dpi	Printing photographs and other images without resizing	24-bit
600 dpi	Printing photographs that will be enlarged by no more than four times the original size	Minimum of 24-bit
1,200 dpi	Printing photographs that will be enlarged more than four times the original size	Minimum of 24-bit

BIT DEPTH, SAY WHAT?

In addition to the resolution, another number that is important when it comes to selecting a scanner is the *bit depth*, also known as *color depth*. This is the number of colors in the digitized image. Actually, bit depth is the number of bits of information needed to record the color information for a single pixel. Usually the higher the bit depth, the better the picture—and the less shading you are likely to get. Ideally to create the richest possible digital duplicates you won't want a scanner that is less than 24-bit. Use any bit depth less than this, and your scanner will show limitations in your images.

Generally, it is better to change the resolution through the scanner, at least until you reach the maximum resolution, before invoking the scanner's interpolated resolution—yes, something else that is found in the documentation that came with your scanner. This means that the native file you begin to work with later on in your graphics program will be at the highest resolution, without

Tip

Important

having asked the scanner to "guess" when it comes to going higher. I often err on the side of too high a resolution to begin with because then, no matter what my project might be, I know that my scanned image is up to it. However, remember that the higher the resolution, the larger the file will be.

Flatbed or photo scanners are probably the best types when it comes to scanning your photographs for a number of reasons. I definitely do not recommend using standard sheetfed scanners for your photos because of the wear and tear they cause. The flatbed system allows you to lay the photo on the glass pane and then close the lid, which helps hold the photo flat during the scanning process. In most cases just the use of the lid keeps the photo flat enough. If it is a particularly damaged photograph or if the scan looks funny—perhaps like a ghost—then it is possible that you may need to lay something slightly heavier on it to force the entire photograph to come in contact with the glass.

Many photo scanners are flatbed scanners as well. From a flexibility standpoint I prefer to find a scanner that offers me many different options without sacrificing quality. If the image quality is poor scanning just doesn't seem worth it. You might want to look for a photo scanner that is a flatbed, to allow for scanning more than just standard-sized photos with a good resolution, but that also offers ways to scan other things, including negatives or microfilm.

In addition to not sacrificing quality, you also don't want to sacrifice the photo you are scanning. Some flatbed-style photo scanners also offer a sheetfed option. If you are interested in getting one of these, remember the way in which the sheetfeed function works in conjunction with the flatbed. The photo is going to be pulled through the feed mechanism and then across the glass plate, where it will stay while the scanning head scans the photo. Then it will be pulled further across the glass and out the other side.

The only kind of sheetfed system I would consider for my photos is one that actually keeps the photo off of the glass plate as it is moving through the system, sitting

---

YOUR SCANNER CAN CHEAT

Through *interpolation,* your scanner's software has found a way to cheat when it comes to resolution. It can fake a higher resolution by making a copy of a nearby pixel. For example, instead of having 1,200 pixels per inch, you may see that the resolution is listed as 2,400 DPI through interpolation. This means each of those 1,200 pixels has one "clone." If you allow the scanner to interpolate, the clarity of your final image is directly related to how good the scanning software's code is for duplicating the pixels.

on the glass only during the actual scanning portion of the process. Even with this system I still would not recommend running older photos through, thus my preference for the flatbed systems with the sheetfed attachment. Finding out if the scanner you are interested in will lift the photo off the glass plate may require an e-mail or telephone call to the sales department of the maker of the scanner before making the purchase.

Photo scanners that use a drawer into which the photo is placed, usually face-up, are generally limited to a $4'' \times 6''$ maximum size photo. Also, the tray may not allow for a warped or otherwise misshaped photo to lie flat during scanning, though the drawer is a nice way to protect your photos during the process. You might want to ask the maker of the scanner if there is something in the inside mechanism that ensures the photo is flat during the scanning process.

The importance of the photo being flat, and thus even, cannot be stressed enough if you are hoping for a quality scan. Even the best graphics programs cannot do the impossible, which is essentially what you are asking it to do when working with a faulty scan.

WHERE SHOULD I PLACE THE PHOTO?

This may seem like a no-brainer, but there are times when the positioning of the photograph on the scanner could affect the outcome. Most flatbed scanners have a preferred corner where they would like you to place the photograph or document. This is usually the upper-right-hand corner if the photograph is placed facedown on the glass (see Figure 3-2 on page 34). This translates to the upper-left corner to the scanner's eye and thus to the computer screen.

While you don't absolutely have to place the photo there, I have found that any time I can push the photograph up against two sides of the part of the scanner that is holding the glass, I get a much straighter scan—another important point to getting the best image.

PREVIEW FIRST

Most scanner software has a preview button or command. It is always a good idea to use this preview option before completing the scan.

The preview does just what you are probably thinking it does; it shows you an example of what the image will look like. In preview mode, regardless of the type of scanner, it will usually do a full scan no matter the size of your original. For a sheetfed this may be the limit of the page, whereas for the flatbed this may be a much larger field since the glass is often slightly wider than a standard $8\frac{1}{2}'' \times 11''$ page and at least an inch longer.

Reminder

HOMEWORK ASSIGNMENT

Don't forget to do your homework before you go to the store to buy any electronics. Being prepared guarantees that you get the best product for your project, regardless of the hype a salesperson may offer about another product.

Reminder

When the preview is shown on the screen, then you have the chance to make sure that the image is straight and that the scan is going to be adequate. You can adjust the size of the selection lines (usually dotted lines) to get just that part of the image you wish to concentrate on when you do the official scan, either to be saved on the hard drive or to be sent directly to your graphics program.

It is here, after you preview the image and before you do the final scan, that you can change the resolution of the output. Depending on how high you make the resolution, it is possible that the scanner software will question your choice, pointing out that all you are doing is making a monster file instead of getting a better image. Of course it tells you this in much more technical terms and is assuming that you are simply scanning the photo to print out. It doesn't take into consideration that you may be planning on enlarging the image or making some other major change that would not be as clear without the higher resolution.

Some people find these notifications annoying. I actually take a moment to read any message box that opens up in any program. I have learned a lot about my computer and specific programs by reading, instead of ignoring, the various messages that pop up. The message boxes are the way your computer tries to communicate with you.

It is also in this preview pane that you will select the area to be used in the final scan. This is an excellent opportunity for you to eliminate part of the photo. Perhaps it is a photo of your grandfather in front of a house, but you

Figure 3-2
Flatbed scanners are easier on photographs because you just place them face down on the glass.

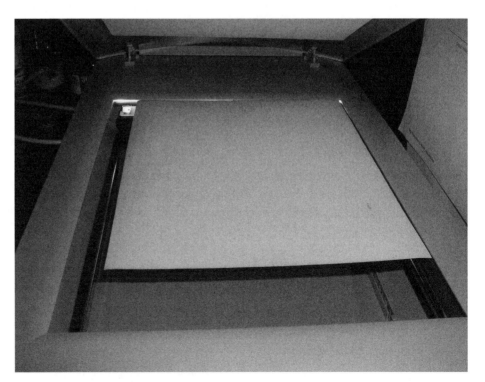

just want his face for use in your genealogy program. Then you would select the area of the image around his face and tell the scanning software to scan again using just the specified section (see Figure 3-3 below). Provided you have not moved or removed the photo from the scanner, the resulting image should be just that portion you have selected.

SCANNING VINTAGE PHOTOGRAPHS

If you are lucky, you may have some tintypes or other antique photos of your ancestors (see Figure 3-4 on page 36). More than contemporary photos, these should be scanned so that you can truly preserve the originals, keeping them out of harm's way.

By their very nature, tintypes cannot be run through a sheetfed scanner of any kind. They might not even fit into photo scanners with a pull-out drawer. In fact, they may be in a case that would be ruined if you tried to remove the photo. So, by process of elimination, you have narrowed down your choice of scanners in this case to a flatbed.

Depending on the condition of the tintype, it may be that you experience shadows or disfigurement in the final image. There may be no way to get around this given the type of photo you are scanning. Instead you will have to be quite patient when it comes to working with the image in the graphics program you have selected.

Warning

COPYRIGHT STILL APPLIES

Remember—just because you can scan letters or family stories that others have shared doesn't mean you can do anything you want with them. Such items usually are covered under the copyright law. Before you use them in any book or publish them on the Internet, don't forget to ask permission of the originator.

Figure 3-3

Once you have digitized a photo you can then use a graphics program, such as Adobe Photoshop, to select just one person's face and create a separate image for use in your genealogy program.

Figure 3-4
Tintypes such as this should always be digitized using a flatbed scanner or a digital camera.

Idea Generator

SCANNING ORIGINAL DOCUMENTS

Another way to use your scanner for preservation is to digitize documents, especially those originals you may have that, even if you do manage to get them replaced, would not be the same.

One of the most important articles to preserve is the family Bible (see Figure 3-5 on page 37). After all, if it disintegrates there is no way to get another copy of it, like so many of the other records we use in our research. The pages of the Bible where the births, marriages, and deaths are recorded are often ornate and rich in color. It would be a shame to lose not only the information but the beauty.

Like the photographs, you probably have many different documents that are beginning to show signs of aging. These need to be digitized first so that

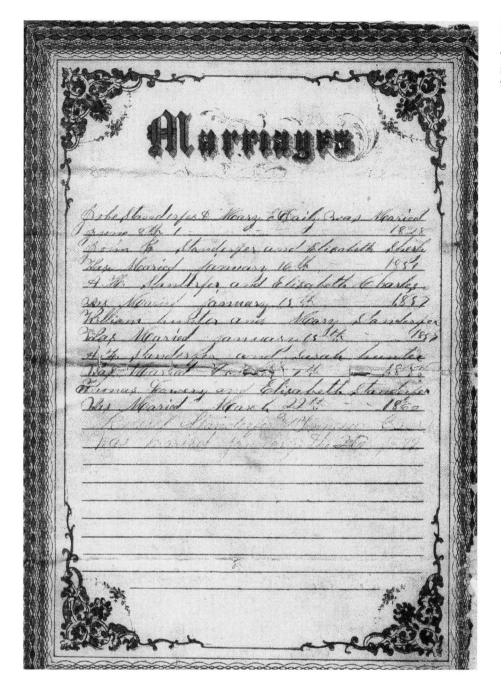

Figure 3-5
Documents can be preserved
with scanners. Bible pages
should be scanned using a
flatbed scanner.

they can be placed in protective sheets and preserved. Then, you can share
the digitized copies with immediate family and distant cousins with no fear
of harming the original.

Some documents easily lend themselves to a sheetfed scanner. If the documents in question contain text, you may want to consider not only scanning
them so you have a digitized duplicate graphic, but also importing the text
through OCR software into a word processing program. This makes it easier
for you to incorporate typed letters, for instance, into a published family history.

When I mention publishing, I am not just talking about books. There are so many different ways to publish now, and when you are looking for mementos and heirlooms to digitize, don't exclude something just because it is in color. If you share your family history on the Internet, then you can publish any images in color.

TAKING MY FOLDERS WITH ME

The problem with genealogy is all the paper we generate or, more aptly, *should* be generating. We should have copies of the records and resources that back up the conclusions we have come to in our research. If you have a notebook computer, it is likely that you have all of your ancestors in a genealogy program that goes with you on research trips. Unfortunately, it has not been possible to take more than a few files of your photocopied records with you at any time, especially if you are flying. **If you have a sheetfed scanner or a sheetfeed adapter for your flatbed scanner, you may want to consider digitizing your backup documents and using your CD-ROM to copy them to CDs to take with you as you travel.**

This can be a labor-intensive project, which is why it really needs to be done using a sheetfed system. Babysitting each page as it is scanned will quickly dim your enthusiasm for taking all your files with you on CDs. Of course, for this system to work, all of your documents or copies need to be no wider than the width of the sheet-feed, for an obvious reason. If you have larger copies, perhaps $11'' \times 17''$ copies of the census, you may need to manually scan these in two sections and then stitch them together using your graphics program.

This is another reason to try to keep your copies all the same size. It makes it much easier to run them through the scanner and to store them on CDs. I have a folder for each couple on my pedigree chart, arranged alphabetically by name of husband. As such, I have carried this over onto CD files, creating a directory (or file folder as it appears in Windows) for each corresponding paper file. I scan all the documents in the same order they are in my paper folders. Since I have an index page at the front of each folder, I also include this in the scan so I can quickly access the records or book pages I need.

BEYOND THE PAPER

Too often we limit our sights to just digitizing documents and photographs. But with the power of today's scanners, there is no limit to what you can scan and add to your electronic family history. And not only do scanners produce higher-quality duplicates than many photocopiers, but they require that you scan each item only once to have it available for printing at any time.

Idea Generator

CD Source

SCAN TO CD

One way to save time when working with a quantity of pages, such as scanning the pages in your folders, is to see if your scanner has a scan-to-CD option. This means that as each page is fed through and scanned, the computer already knows you want to save it to a disk in the CD-ROM. This is a great time saver—it can be scanning up to thirty or thirty-five pages (depending on the capacity of the sheet-fed adapter) while you are doing something else.

When you scan the pages of your family Bible, don't forget to scan the actual cover of the Bible. Just as the pages inside may have been designed for beauty, the cover may reveal an entirely different history. Depending how old the Bible is, the scratches, indentations, or just general wear of the cover may bring back fond memories for you or other family members. Perhaps you fondly remember walking to church with the Bible clutched in your arms.

It is also important to scan the title page so that anyone viewing the information can see the copyright date and can tell if the records written on the pages are contemporary or later additions.

Going Beyond Photos and Papers

Even clothing and material can be scanned. While we will talk about these items in more detail when we look at cameras later in chapter six, there are times when the scanner may give you another view. If your family is lucky enough to have a tartan that has been handed down, you would certainly want to take pictures of it to show what the entire garment looked like, but scanning a portion of the tartan would give you an upclose image of the actual pattern of the fabric. The image then could be manipulated further, but since it was a high-quality zoomed scan, it would be easier to work with and would not lose any definition as you work in a graphics program.

Idea Generator

NEEDLEPOINT ART

While taking a photograph of any needlepoint work that may have been handed down is one way to preserve it, I like to use my scanner to get the best of images. The high resolution of the scanner allows me to enlarge or shrink the image—and it still can be printed out on photo paper. The scanner offers the chance to digitize all the intricate details of such a true work of art, right down to the fiber of the material on which it was sewn.

A TRULY PERSONAL WEB SITE

Once you have scanned the fabric or tartan, you could use it as the background image of the family history Web page. Consider how personal that page would be to your cousins, especially when they understand the significance of that design. You could even adopt it as the "wallpaper"—background image—of your desktop computer. Once it has been digitized, there is no limit to what you can do with the file.

Other family heirlooms can be similarly scanned and included in published family histories, or you could print out photographic quality prints to share with relatives far and near.

But what about slides? If your family had slides made of family trips or other occasions you may be wondering how hard it is to work with those, or perhaps you have some negatives to which you no longer have original photographs. **Through specialized scanners or attachments to your flatbed, there are ways to create wonderful images of slides and negatives, as well as microfilm, if you have a little patience.**

Idea Generator

FOUR

Digitizing Slides and Negatives

U p to this point we have focused on digitizing traditional photos and documents, but many of us probably have a ton of negatives and slides that need to be preserved as well. You may think that scanning slides and negatives is the same as scanning photographs. While the process is similar, the need to use a transparency adapter raises some unique issues. The image that results can be dependent on how the adapter renders the slide or negative viewable for the scanner and adjustments for color and clarity. This is why I suggest familiarizing yourself with your scanner by starting with a few of your better traditional photos, so you can see how changing the settings affects the scanned image. When you use the adapter, you have to know how to change settings to get the best possible image from the slide or negative.

FILM SCANNER VS. TRANSPARENCY ADAPTED FLATBED

If you have decided to select one of the specialty film scanners that use a tray or insert to handle the slides or negatives, remember that it can't scan other media. Many of them will not be able to scan microfilm either, as the tray is limited to the length of a standard negative strip, and the extra-long microfilm couldn't be fed in.

Scanners devoted to slides and negatives are designed to scan in the best possible quality, with high resolution. They often have a higher price tag, as well, primarily because the companies that make such scanners cater to professional photographers who expect the best images possible—and are willing to pay for them. For what genealogists do with the images, though, it may not be necessary to commit that much money to your project.

You already know that I think the transparency adapter that is available for many of the flatbed scanners is the way to go, considering money, space, and flexibility issues. After all, we only have so much space in our office and on our desk for computer peripherals. A scanner that offers a variety of functionality means getting the most for our money, something that we must consider given that genealogy for most of us is just a hobby.

While scanners devoted to slides and negatives often cost in the upper hundreds of dollars range, flatbed scanners with transparency adapters that can be plugged in or that come built into the lid of the scanner range in price from less than one hundred dollars to about four hundred dollars, depending on the model and the brand. Of course, as we so often remind ourselves after we have "saved a bundle," we get what we pay for. **Going for the least expensive may not be the best approach with these scanners.** It is more important to compare what you are getting with each one. The eighty dollar scanner may end up being more expensive once you realize you have to purchase the needed adapter separately.

Reminder

AN INTRODUCTION TO SCANNING SLIDES

Perhaps the biggest difference between slides or negatives and traditional photographs is the resolution needed for the scan. In the last chapter you learned what resolutions are needed for traditional photo scanning. In gen-

BIGGER IS BETTER, RIGHT?

We have been raised to believe certain fallacies, one of which is the adage "bigger is better." This isn't always the case, especially when it comes to working with digitized images. There is an upper limit to which you can enlarge an image before it stops being better and is just bigger.

As we've discussed, scanning converts an image into small dots or pixels. That is what resolution is all about. The higher the number, the more dots or pixels are created per inch. If the resolution is 300 DPI and the initial image in the computer is 4″×6″, that means the digitized image is 1,200 dots×1,800 dots. Many people think that when they enlarge the picture they are getting more dots per inch. While there are ways to do this in graphics software, many overlook that necessary step. Instead they are taking those 1,200×1,800 dots and spreading them out over a larger area, perhaps an 8″×10″ space. This only makes the dots bigger.

It is the fact that the dots are bigger that makes you more aware of them when you print the image. This is usually what makes people unhappy with the conversion of their clear photographs to a digital alternative.

eral, most photographs could be adequately reprinted at 300 DPI. However, when it comes to slides or negatives, this isn't high enough, so in addition to looking for a scanner that can be purchased for a reasonable price, you also must make sure that the scanner will do what you need it to when it comes to digitizing slides or negatives.

Don't make the mistake of limiting your scanning resolution by basing it on your printer's output resolution. Though it is likely that you eventually will be printing the image, the initial scan has little to do with the printer. It has more to do with the fact that the negative or slide is quite small when you scan it, and, therefore, it is likely that you will be enlarging the images before you send them to the printer.

Unlike the 4″ × 6″ photograph, each slide or negative is only about 6 square centimeters. The final print may be upwards of ten times that size, and any time you enlarge an image to that extent there are things you need to keep in mind.

Most important is that the resolution must be higher than when working with a regular photograph. The higher the resolution, the more pixels or dots there are per inch. The more pixels per inch (PPI), the more flexibility is available when it comes to enlarging or making other changes to the image, thus avoiding artifacts in the image on the computer.

Reminder

Low scanner resolutions do not allow you to enlarge the image because the enlargement makes the graininess of the picture more pronounced. You would not be happy with the outcome and certainly would not want to share the image with family.

One of the reasons it took a long time for me to embrace the digital world

ARTIFACTS

Artifacts are any noise, blurring, jagged edges, or other abnormality that degrades the digital image. These artifacts are introduced at the time the image is converted into a digital format as a result of the limitations of the computer. Unlike the "real world," where there is the possibility of infinite variability, computer hardware has self-imposed limits on variability. This is especially true when it comes to colors and resolution. There are only so many cells to a scanner head, thus limiting the total number of dots per inch, for instance. Likewise, there are only so many colors the computer can recognize. Even though that number is in the millions with the newest products, it is still a limitation, and the picture in question may have a color that the scanner or computer cannot handle. When this happens, it grabs the next closest shade. For example, if you scan a picture of the sunset, the scanned image might not have as flawless a fading of the sky's colors as the original photo did. This effect is known as *banding*.

for photos, and the use of scanners beyond simple projects, was the graininess. I wanted the clarity of a traditional 35mm photo in my digital counterparts, and I wasn't willing to settle for less. When I say I wanted clarity, that means I expected it even when I practically had my nose touching the printed picture, not just when it was further away, say at arms length.

LET THERE BE LIGHT

Without the backlight of the transparency adapter, when the scanner makes a pass along the slide or negative strip, the scanner only sees a dark blob. It is the light that renders the slide or negative readable. Remember, as the scanner's head passes by, it shoots out and records the light, converting the current.

Transparency adapters come in different formats now. Some are large square ones, usually about 7″ × 8″ in size. These often have a special connection so that you can hook them up to the scanner only when you need them. The accompanying scanning software recognizes when the adapter has been plugged into the scanner and offers appropriate choices in addition to the more traditional flatbed scanning options.

If the scanner is a flatbed with an adapter, you might need to individually select each slide to be scanned and saved (see Figure 4-1 on page 44). By utilizing the drag option on your mouse, you should be able to start at the upper-left-hand corner and highlight the image on the slide or negative. It is a good idea to select the image just inside the slide's frame or just inside the negative's picture. This will give you a better image to work with in a graphics program or when printing it out. A similar approach can be used with any document or photograph you scan. This is yet another way you need to experiment with your scanner to see how changing the selected scanning area adjusts some of the other defaults.

While your scanner software may allow you to zoom in on the desired scanning area, this does not mean the final scanned image will be enlarged. Enlargement—as well as methods for fixing or enhancing the image—is usually done within a graphics program. It is always better to use the program that is best suited to a task, and in this case, it is not the scanning program but the graphics programs, which is discussed in chapter eight.

Internet Source

DIY

If you want to try your hand at making your own transparency adapter, see "How to Scan 35mm Slides on a Flatbed Scanner" online at <www.abstractconcretewo rks.com/essays/scanning/ Backlighter.html>.

HOW BIG ARE YOUR NEGATIVES?

If the scanner you have selected has a built-in backlight in the cover, then your ability to scan slides or negatives is limited to this single strip. I mention this because I have quite a few negatives that are actually individual pictures and measure about 2″ × 3½″ in size. Unlike the transparency adapter that is placed over the negative and has a solid backlight source measuring at least

Definitions

MASK

A *mask* is any filter used to block something, whether it is data or, in the case of scanning slides, the backlight. The masking is designed to control where the backlight shows through. With a slide or negative, the mask focuses the light on that slide or negative so the scanner reproduces an image rather than a dark blob.

$4'' \times 4''$, and probably bigger, these other backlights are predesigned specifically for a single negative strip or about four slides.

While the majority of your negatives and slides would be served by the built-in backlight, you will find it is not wide enough to scan larger negatives and it is too wide to scan the negatives for panoramic pictures produced by cameras like the Kodak Advantix, which uses 24mm film. With panoramic negatives, a full 11mm around the negative leaves the backlight exposed during the scan. This additional light exposure will affect the final image.

This may be an even bigger issue with scanners into which you feed the negative strip or in which you set the strip in a drawer. Because they are designed for a specific purpose, they may not be able to handle any variations of standard negatives. While the resolution on these specialty scanners is always higher, the flatbed with the transparency adapter is a more flexible tool.

HIDING BEHIND A MASK

One way to control the leaking of light is through the use of masking. If you have a flatbed scanner with a transparency adapter, it is likely that it came

Figure 4-1
With the transparency adapter lighting the negatives, the scanner can digitize the selected image which can then be inverted through graphics software.

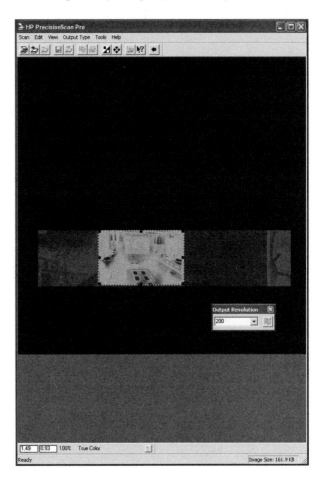

STRAY LIGHT

If some of the transparency adapter's light leaks around the slide or negative, it will affect the scanned image. As the scanner head passes over the slide, it isn't smart enough to recognize that it is a slide. Instead, it is throwing out and reading the light from the scanner head as it bounces off of everything. When it comes in contact with the light bleeding in from the transparency adapter, it may react to it and affect the entire scan. It is important to ensure that no direct light is peaking through around the sides of the slide or negative when scanning.

---

with a few precut "maskings" to aid in placement of a negative strip or of four slides. The masking fits snuggly around the slide or negative strip to prevent light from leaking through as the scanner makes its pass, thus preventing any distortion or color changes in the digitized image.

While the standard sizes of masking resemble the backlight strip of other scanners in that they are designed to support the 35mm negative strip or the 35mm slides, this does not mean you are limited to these. Although these precut maskings are usually sturdier and easier to use—simply drop a slide in each of the four slots in the slide masking—you actually can make your own maskings to support odd-sized or panoramic negatives.

One of the best ways, and certainly the most inexpensive, is to take a piece of black construction paper and make the appropriate cutout (see Figure 4-2 on page 46). When I am creating a new masking, I lay down the negative or slide in question and use a white pen to mark the outer edges of the strip or slide. I then cut along the inside of the lines I have drawn, giving myself a small margin on the inside. I would rather have to cut more than start over. By working with an inside margin, I always can enlarge it if it is not quite wide enough yet.

Rather than using scissors to do the cutting, I use a small plexi-board—actually intended for quilting—and an X-Acto knife. This way I do not run the risk of bending the paper during the cutting process. It is important that the paper be flat against the glass of the flatbed scanner and that it hugs the edges of the negative in question to prevent the leaking of the transparency light.

Tip

Each masking you cut should be done from a separate piece of construction paper. Remember that the point of the masking is to let in backlight only where the negative in question is sitting. As such I tend to limit each sheet to a single space for the negative in question, usually in the center of the piece of paper. I also make sure to write on the back side of the masking, the side that isn't facedown on the glass, what size slide or negative it has been cut to fit. This saves me time in the future when I don't have to guess whether

Figure 4-2
If your scanner's supplied masks do not fit the negatives you have, you can use black construction paper to create your own.

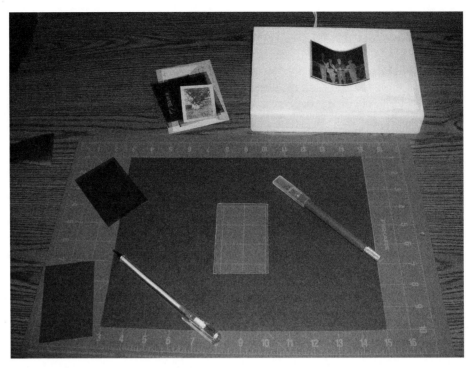

or not I have selected the masking of the appropriate size. I store all of my self-made maskings in a manila folder to protect them from being torn or bent. The less there is for the scanner to see on the construction paper, the better my scan of the negative will be.

Provided your flatbed scanner is designed to handle images up to 8½″ × 11″, you should be able to create maskings for any size negative, glass plate, or other item that requires a backlight to be scanned.

If you have a smaller slide scanner with a built-in backlight in the lid, you still may be able to make your own masking—at least for a negative strip that is thinner than 35mm. For those oddly shaped ones that are bigger, you will be out of luck, because there will be no way to get an even scan. Even if the scanner does see the edges that extend beyond the backlight strip, only the center will be properly lit.

If you are using a film scanner that requires you to feed the negative strip through a slot in the front, then you can't scan anything that isn't a 35mm negative strip or a 35mm slide. I stress the limitation of this type of scanner, because many consumers are attracted to its high resolution despite its sometimes equally high price tag. I think many genealogists may find themselves disappointed in this type of scanner if they are trying to digitize any odd-sized or -shaped negatives or slides.

WHAT ABOUT MICROFILM?

When I went out looking for a new scanner—the color one I had purchased sometime ago was no longer meeting my needs, though it was still a workhorse—I was not yet familiar with transparency adapters. I was impressed with how thin some of the scanners were, but had not followed my own advice that day: I had not already researched the current crop of scanners and the new features that were available, so I didn't know ahead of time which scanner I wanted.

As my husband and I were looking at one particular model, he pointed to the one next to it and mentioned the transparency adapter. I had to have the concept of the adapter explained to me, which he did patiently. It wasn't until I got it home and began to take the pieces out of the box that the masking for the 35mm negative strip got me to thinking. If it could handle a 35mm negative strip, shouldn't it be able to handle 35mm microfilm?

Having purchased a number of microfilms of family histories, censuses and other information throughout the years (before much of it became available on the Internet), **I was curious if I could use my scanner as a microfilm copier.** I still didn't see the big picture—scanning to the computer and using the image on my computer. But I decided to try scanning the microfilm and see what happened.

Step By Step

I used my microfilm reader to find an appropriate page, and then I carefully tried to feed the appropriate section of the microfilm into the predesigned masking for 35mm negative strips. This was quite a lesson in persistence, as the 35mm negative strip masking had a lip designed to hold the strip firmly to prevent any light from leaking in from the transparency adapter. And then there were the clumsy microfilm reels that I had to lay on either side of the scanner. This often threw off the image on the microfilm I was trying to scan by twisting or pulling at the film. The microfilm reels kept tipping on their sides or, if I was completely unlucky for the day, rolling off the desk and unraveling into microfilm spaghetti on the floor.

It wasn't until recently that I solved the dilemma of the tipping and rolling reels by using microfilm boxes. By placing a box on either side of the flatbed scanner I found I could support the reels while still forcing the necessary section of the microfilm to lay flat in the masking so that I could make the scan. While it is still not a perfect system, it does allow me to scan images I find on the census, which I can then print, link in my genealogy program, or burn to a CD.

For More Info

GUIDE TO THE FHL

To find out more about the Family History Library, see *Your Guide to the Family History Library* by Paula Stuart Warren and James W. Warren (Cincinnati: Betterway Books, 2001).

Another way I have simplified this process is by creating a custom masking for the microfilm. Because there is no lip, it is much easier to use, as I am no longer fighting to get the correct section of the microfilm into the small area that will be scanned. But, because there is no lip, I must be extremely careful to line up the edges of the microfilm with the edges of the masking and to make sure it stays there during the entire scanning process. To solve this I undercut the masking a bit so there is a little overlap between the masking and the microfilm.

This certainly should be considered the poor man's approach to scanning microfilm, at least in a genealogist's office, but sometimes we have to work with what we have, including the dollars we can spend on this hobby. Microfilm scanners are expensive, though the quality is certainly better than the method I have described here. Specialty microfilm scanners use lenses that zoom in on the image in question, making it easier to read and requiring no size manipulation.

Reminder

The Family History Library in Salt Lake City, Utah, offers microfilm scanners on each of the research floors: United States/Canada (second floor), International (Basement 1), and British Isles (Basement 2). With these powerful machines you can make high-quality scans, which you can then use in your family history or upload to a Web site, provided the data in the images from the microfilm is not protected under copyright law. This is also a great way to save money or gather images from a tax book or other county book that may require reading page-by-page. Scanning it to CD and then taking it home allows you to search it at your leisure, rather than trying to go through the film at the library. However, there are limitations to what you can scan. Just as they have warnings about copying complete books, because it violates copyright laws, they also have signs near the scanners explaining the rules regarding digitizing an entire reel of microfilm.

While I would love to have such a scanner in my office, the cost of such machines has tempered my enthusiasm for the time being. Those found in repositories such as the Family History Library are high-end models, and some even have multiple lenses, offering the ability to scan not only 35mm but also the 16mm high-magnification rolls as well.

Notes

SCANNING MICROFILM

The ScanPro Direct Digital Microfilm Reader Printer offers genealogists a way to directly scan microfilm. It is not an option for everyone—it's currently priced in the thousands—but the resulting digitized images are high quality.

Returning to my poor man's method, because the microfilm is so small, it is important to scan at the highest native resolution—that is, the highest DPI possible without using the scanner's interpolation—the scanner can handle. Remember—any time you need to enlarge the image, the scan has to be a higher resolution. Because the image on the microfilm is so small, enlargement is not just an option, but a requirement.

Photo-specific flatbeds are the best for scanning microfilm, as most of them offer up to 4,800 DPI scanning with 48-bit color. This ensures that the clarity and color of the image are preserved. While microfilm is usually black and white, sometimes higher color depth brings out something that was difficult to read on the original microfilm.

DOING THE MATH

You can determine the resolution the slide, negative, or microfilm needs to be scanned at by taking the print resolution and multiplying it by the amount of enlargement that will be necessary to get a properly sized print. For instance, if you want to take a single 35mm slide and make an 11″ × 17″ print—an exaggeration in genealogy, I know—then the enlargement would be ten times the size of original. To print a 360 DPI quality print then would require

---

DOWNSAMPLING

It is possible to scan an image at too high of a resolution. Just as bigger isn't always better, higher isn't always better, at least when it comes to printing. Remember that the resolution of your printer will affect the outcome, just as the original scanned resolution does. Scanning at a high resolution and down-sampling is different from scanning at a lower resolution. Downsampling is the eliminating of pixels. Unlike scanning at the lower resolution, in which each pixel retains the "detail" picked up during the scan, downsampling averages those pixels, thus eliminating some of the texture. If you downsample too much, the resulting image will not have any of the detail of the original.

---

that the original resolution of the slide be 3,600 DPI (360 DPI times ten).

Given that most of what you are likely to do would not require such a heavy enlargement, the highest probably being an 8½″×11″ image, then you may never have to scan as high as 3,600 DPI. I like having the ability though, just in case. Yes, my family has been through both the Girl Scout and Boy Scout programs and believes in the being prepared motto. My computer and the peripherals that I purchase for it are supposed to help me, not hinder me. Getting the highest scanning resolution available and the most flexibility for the most reasonable price is part of the measuring stick I use in selecting my purchase.

THE BEST OF BOTH WORLDS

Of course, as we have seen with the different types of scanners and unique documents and items that genealogists may want to digitize, that measuring stick had many other requirements. While film scanners offer a higher resolution, they are more limited in the things I can scan, even when it comes to negatives and strips.

Genealogy is as much a hobby of adapting as it is of researching. We adapt everything to aid us in our research, and computers and peripherals are no exception. But with adapting comes compromise. Being able to digitize my microfilm or larger older negatives means looking for a scanner that may be a slightly lower resolution, but that offers me more options in what and how I can scan. Fortunately, with the release of photo-specific flatbed scanners, I have a lot of flexibility.

Remember when selecting your scanner that the transparency adapter may be one of the most important features. If you have glass plate negatives or oversized negatives, or want to play around with digitizing microfilm without spending a mint, then you need a transparency adapter that has flexibility. This means

Reminder

choosing a scanner that offers large adapters, rather than one that has the single-slide adapter or the transparency light built into the lid of the scanner.

I'M ALREADY DIGITIZED

A few years back Kodak began to offer Photo CDs with their processed images. Some people I know even sent in their 35mm slides and negatives and had them digitized onto Photo CDs when this whole concept was brand new. You may find that your genealogy software has a special menu option for inserting a picture from a Photo CD. You may even be excited that you elected to go this route yourself with a roll of film, looking forward to all the ways you will be able to use the images with your computer.

While there is certainly nothing wrong with getting photos processed onto CDs, you may find that the resolution leaves something to be desired. Like so many other aspects of genealogy, we must understand why the system is in place. Just as we have to understand why we get certain information from a vital record or why the census was taken only every ten years (given that they didn't consult with genealogists), we also must understand the thinking behind the photo CD process.

In a nutshell, this process originally was invented to display photos through your television set. Sounds fine. The problem is that your television set is a much lower resolution than your computer or your printer, so the images on the CD are also at a much lower resolution—and as we have already seen, resolution with digitized images is everything.

Fortunately, today's Photo CDs offer more for the consumer. Multiple resolutions are available for each picture on the CD, allowing you to have both a lower resolution version, which is easy to open on the computer and may be appropriate for uploading to the Web, and also a high resolution version, which is ideal for printing quality photos. You can find out all there is to know about Kodak's CD processing by visiting <www.kodak.com>. Be sure that you are looking at information about the Photo CD. This is more expensive than the Picture Disk they offer, but is the only way to guarantee that you get the higher resolution images.

MOVING ON

While many people still have their 35mm cameras, the cost of digital cameras has come down considerably in the last couple of years, and the quality has continued to improve. Digital cameras are being purchased like never before, and many genealogists are making the leap to these new gadgets right along with the rest of the world. Understanding what the digital camera offers— and the pitfalls that need to be avoided—is essential to making sure your purchase is the best one for your needs.

Notes

WORKING WITH PHOTO CDs

If you have a number of photo CDs, you may want to investigate SilverFast Pho-toCD software <www.silver fast.com>. This software easily accesses the photos on the CD and includes some auto-adjust features that ensure you don't have to be a photography expert to get a good image from the file on the CD.

FIVE

An Introduction to Digital Photography

W ith the abundance of inexpensive 35mm film cameras, including disposable ones, why is everyone flocking toward digital cameras? What is all the excitement? Are they really any better than the traditional film cameras? What should you know about digital cameras before you get one? And finally, do you really need one?

I am one of the first to admit that for quite some time, while I had a digital camera, I also saw serious limitations in it—most noticeably when it came to printing the pictures I had taken. I have come to the conclusion that I am a detail-oriented person, and perhaps that is where some of my children get it. When my son was in kindergarten and he came home around Thanksgiving and told me the story of the Mayflower and the Pilgrims, I was struck by one comment he made. He was the only one of my four children to mention that the Pilgrims got into a little boat before stepping on the famous Plymouth Rock. I wonder where he gets his concern for detail—when it came to viewing the photos I printed with that first digital camera I had, I didn't see the picture because I was staring at all the pixels that were clearly visible in the photo. And the pixilation of the photo bothered me so much that it was years before I even ventured to print another one.

Since that time I have had two more digital cameras. As the technology improves, each camera I purchase offers me more, as do the printers I use to print them on. I now can say that the photos I print are as high-quality with the digital as anything I could do with a regular 35mm film camera.

Internet Source

BEGINNER'S LUCK

Not sure where to begin with a digital camera? Check out BetterPhoto.com <www.betterphoto.com/digital.asp>.

SO WHAT'S THE BIG DEAL THEN?

If the digital camera produces photos equally good to the ones I took with a traditional camera, then what is all the hoopla? For me, the digital camera's biggest advantage over traditional cameras has got to be allowing me to check my handiwork before leaving the scene. Too often I have gotten my prints back from the photo store only to discover that I chopped off part of Aunt Rhody's head or that the tombstone I thought was quite legible was in fact covered in shadows that made it harder than ever to read the inscription—the inscription I elected not to write down because I had taken the picture.

When George Eastman, founder of Kodak, introduced his portable Kodak camera in 1888, his slogan was "You press the button, we do the rest." For years this was truly how it worked. You pressed the button, and then you let someone else develop the prints and hoped all would go well. Provided the camera operator (you or I) did a good job of taking the pictures, then usually all did go well, and you could ooh and aah at your new pictures of the cute new baby or marvel years later at how the children had grown.

GEORGE EASTMAN AND KODAK

George Eastman is synonymous with Kodak, and he should be. He not only founded the company, but the Kodak name was his own invention, springing out of his love for the letter K. George was born 12 July 1854 in Waterville, N.Y., which is near Utica, to George Washington Eastman, who first ran a nursery and then established Eastman Commercial College, and his wife, Maria Kilbourn. Eastman's goal was to "make the camera as convenient as the pencil."

It's been a long time coming, but I would say that cameras are definitely getting there. And that is in no small part due to the inventions of George Eastman. Perhaps he knew that genealogists one day would want to immortalize tombstones or would be eternally grateful for the photos that survive of great-grandmother. But then, what else could we expect of a descendant of the first governor of Plymouth Colony?

Yes, George Eastman's ancestry can be traced back to Governor William Bradford, among other prominent movers and shakers of early Colonial New England. Eastman is Bradford's sixth great-grandson.

Eastman had dreams of the camera being an extension of the public, used as much as, say, the pencil. Of course, given the time lag between taking the picture and receiving the prints, not to mention the costs involved in developing those prints, this just wasn't an option. The digital camera has truly brought Eastman's dream much closer to reality. While I won't say that I take my digital camera with me everywhere, I will say that when I go on any trip it is often at the top of my list, whereas in the past it was more often an afterthought if I had room in the bag.

Size, ability, and ease of use all have played a part in my conversion to a true digital photo enthusiast. My first digital camera saved images to a floppy disk.

Most of our notebook computers don't even have this antiquated storage device anymore, and though some desktop computers still have one, I would guess few of us really use it anymore. At the time, the idea of storing to floppy disk seemed like a major plus in my book. This meant as long as I had floppies with me, I had unlimited picture-taking opportunities. Of course, the limited technology of the time also meant my digital camera was a hefty little machine rather than something that could be tucked into the back pocket of my jeans. So while I had this unlimited storage ability, I didn't always take the camera with me because it was bulky and saving the pictures to the floppy disks took time.

That first camera wasn't even a 1-megapixel camera. My next one was a 3.3-megapixel model that was quite a bit smaller. I used this camera for at least three years, enjoying the fact that it saved images to compact flash cards; this meant that as long as I had more than one compact flash card, I had unlimited digital film of sorts. This year I decided to do it up right and went with a high-end 5-megapixel model that offers slots for more than one type of medium, which means I don't have to change the cards as frequently as they get filled. While it's physically bigger than my 3.3 was, the new camera has many features that make it more like a traditional film camera while giving me the benefits of digital. And it is one of the first things I make sure I have room for in my bags whenever I travel. I never know when I will get a chance to visit a cemetery, after all.

Don't worry if all of the technical terms seem a little like "geek speak" to you right now. You are about to be introduced to all of these concepts so you will have an overview of the different types of cameras available and how varying properties and features can affect the process of taking pictures as well as your possible satisfaction with the finished products.

Notes

The latest technology in digital photography, coupled with the falling prices, leaves few cons to adding a digital camera to your list of other genealogy essentials. There are many ways to share these pictures that are less difficult or expensive than traditional film processing, and you'll always know whether or not you got the picture you were after immediately after you take it. Perhaps the only con is that it may be less difficult to use than a traditional point-and-click camera. Actually, as you will see in this chapter, there are a number of point-and-click digital cameras that can be operated much like the traditional ones.

A CAMERA IS A CAMERA, RIGHT?

There are a number of different types of digital cameras. And perhaps it is this vast number of choices that prevents some people from picking one. They are sure that they will pick the wrong one or that, once they have picked, it will become obsolete before they leave the store. Given that a digital camera

Definitions

MEGAPIXEL

A *megapixel* is actually 1,048,576 pixels. And a pixel is a single dot. The megapixel as it is used with the camera indicates the quality of the image. The higher the megapixel number, the clearer the ultimate photo will be and the more flexibility you will have with what you can do with that image, including enlarging it.

Figure 5-1
Intermediate cameras, such as the Canon Powershot, offer flexibility, LCD screens, and point-and-shoot capabilities.

is something like a computer, there is some truth to this concern. But just like your computer, if you think through what you want to do with the camera before you select one, you will find that even if it is obsolete by "geek" standards, it is still giving you great pictures and doing everything you need.

Most books and articles on digital cameras break them down into the following groups based on megapixels and price. So in keeping with other information you are likely to find as you further investigate these products, I have grouped them in the same manner.

- Web cams are inexpensive—okay, cheap—little cameras that attach to your computer and allow you to view and record images or movies. They are not even 1-megapixel models and are completely unsuitable for the projects genealogists use a camera for.
- Point-and-click—usually fall in the 1.3- to 2-megapixel range and have a price tag of between one and two hundred dollars. They are usually small in physical size, but may limit you in the number of pictures and the amount of internal storage they can handle.
- Intermediate—offer 2- to 4-megapixel resolutions and cost from two to five hundred dollars. They come equipped with a zoom feature and some storage card capability, offering you expandable digital film abilities (see Figure 5-1 below).

- Advanced Consumer—have increased resolution of 5 to 6 megapixels and a higher price of between five and nine hundred dollars. There are a lot more bells and whistles with this group, including some manual settings that resemble those of traditional film cameras (see Figure 5-2 on page 55).
- Prosumer—are usually 6 megapixels, perhaps higher, and cost anywhere from one to three thousand dollars. These are intended for serious hobbyists and for some professionals, and offer many settings, extended features, and more of what true photographers need in a camera.
- Professional—high-end cameras with 8 megapixels or above, some with as many as 16 megapixels. Of course, professional models have the price tag to match the features, usually costing more than five thousand dollars.

They are rugged—capable of handling the abuse of a traveling professional photographer—and they take pictures fast, allowing the professional to click off picture after picture as he would with a high-end film camera.

It is likely that you will find yourself naturally gravitating to those cameras found in the point-and-click and intermediate classes because of size and price. Some of you may find that you want the power of those in the advanced consumer category and are willing to pay more for those features.

Figure 5-2
Advanced consumer cameras, such as the Olympus 5050C, more closely resemble traditional 35mm cameras and offer lots of manual settings in addition to point-and-shoot automation.

IT'S A MATTER OF MEGAPIXELS

While we have been taught, with just about everything that involves images and resolutions, that the bigger the numbers the better, when it comes to picking the right camera, this is not always the case. **You need to look at a number of factors, including features and limitations of the camera.** You also need to consider what you plan to do with the photos in question.

Important

For genealogists, there are certain types of projects that we seem to find ourselves regularly involved in. Some involve taking pictures, while others involve sharing them. If you primarily want to print images to standard $4'' \times 6''$ prints or share them on the Web, you will find that the camera options available to you are greatly increased, as is the flexibility of the price of the cameras.

Remember that you can always get a camera with a higher resolution than you think you might need. It is always better to have more than to have less to ensure that you get the quality that you expected. This table illustrates the least expensive category based on the project and the minimum megapixels needed to complete that project.

POINT-AND-CLICK VS. EXTRA FEATURES

Before you can decide on whether to stick with a point-and-click camera or look into going up a category and paying for a few extra features, you need

Project	Minimum Number of Megapixels	Camera Category
Enlarging images from 4″×6″ to 8″×10″ or 11″×17″	3.3 to 6	Intermediate and Advanced Consumer
Cropping a part of a photo and enlarging it to full photo size	3.3 to 6	Intermediate and Advanced Consumer
Creating slide shows to display on the computer (for a family reunion)	2 to 4	Intermediate
Creating a PowerPoint presentation	2 to 4	Intermediate
Printing 4″×6″ photos	2 to 4	Point-and-Click and Intermediate
Publishing to the Web	1.3	Point-and-Click

to be honest about what you want to do with the camera and about how experienced you are with cameras in general. It is also a good idea to consider how comfortable you would be with a camera that could require decisions and adjustments on your part. If you find yourself using disposable film cameras because all you have to do is point at the subject and press a button, then you will find the point-and-click digital cameras more to your liking, and will be likely to get more use out of it in the long run.

Reminder

While cost is often a deciding factor with any big purchase we make, **if you find that the features of a slightly more expensive camera will serve your purposes, then you may want to save up for that one rather than settling for a cheaper one that doesn't have everything you want or need.** Genealogists usually think hard about how much they will use such products in their genealogy hobby before purchasing them. We sometimes spend a little more money in the beginning to get a better product that we know will last a little longer, thus getting the better value in the end. Cameras are no exception to this.

KEY FEATURES WHEN DECIDING ON A CAMERA

Many people base their digital camera selections simply on the number of megapixels the camera offers, but there are many other aspects to consider that might directly affect both your experience with the camera and the resulting pictures. These include:

- Lens requirements
- Sensor resolution
- Exposure controls
- Flash options
- Viewfinder options
- Storage options

- Batteries
- Ease of use

Lens Requirements

Beginning with the intermediate category cameras, those that have 2 to 4 megapixels, zoom options become available (see Figure 5-3 below). Sometimes two types of zoom functions are mentioned in the specifications for the camera: optical and digital. Few people understand that there is a difference between these two zooms.

The optical zoom is closer to the zoom ability on a traditional 35mm camera. The lens is designed to magnify the image, thus giving you a close-up of the subject in question. The optical zoom does this mechanically by adjusting the optical elements—the glass or plastic pieces of the lens that focus the light. The more optical elements the camera has, the better the chance for optical zoom abilities. Digital cameras usually display this zoom ability as a 3x zoom or a 4x zoom. This number tells you that the lens zooms in at a range that triples (3x) or quadruples (4x) itself.

The digital zoom, on the other hand, is a way of taking a 4x zoom and perhaps doubling or tripling that zoom digitally. So if the camera specifications say the camera had a 4x optical zoom and a 2x digital zoom, that means the camera has the capacity to shoot an 8x zoom.

The way in which the digital zoom works actually may cause more problems with your image than it solves. You see, the digital zoom interpolates the image. Much as the scanners we talked about estimate or duplicate pixels

Figure 5-3
The optical zoom function allows you to get up close so you can view minute details.

when they interpolate to get a higher resolution, the camera estimates the center pixels of the image to enlarge it. The problem is that as the camera does this it sometimes causes distortions in the picture.

I use the digital zoom on my camera from time to time and have not experienced such a distortion, but the quality of my camera might have something to do with that. Less expensive cameras may not produce such high-quality results with the interpolation, resulting in images that are pixilated when you try to print or enlarge them. Also, if you enlarge images shot with the digital zoom, you will definitely see more distortions than are normal.

Sensor Resolution

Resolution is where you get the megapixel rating for a camera, and most of the time the higher the megapixel rating the better the camera—and the resolution. Many other factors, such as the zoom feature mentioned above, may directly affect the final picture, but you can equate the resolutions of a digital camera basically along these lines. One-megapixel cameras are considered low-resolution models. Some 2- and all of the 3.3- to 4-megapixel cameras offer medium resolutions. Finally, anything 5 megapixels and higher produces high-resolution images.

RESOLUTION NAME TO PIXEL RESOLUTION	
Resolution Name	**Pixel Resolution**
Economy/VGA	640 × 480 pixels (low)
Standard/SVGA	1,024 × 768 pixels (medium)
Fine/SXGA	1,280 × 960 pixels (medium)
Superfine/UXGA	1,600 × 1,200 pixels (high)
High	2,048 × 1,536 pixels (high)

If you are uploading pictures to the Web, it is not necessary to have a high-resolution image. Computer monitors can only handle so much, and the files get exponentially bigger depending on the resolution. So when publishing images to the Web it is a good idea to at least upload the first image in a low resolution, perhaps with a link to a higher-resolution image if there is intricate detail that you want your site's visitors to see.

All of today's cameras offer a way to select a reduced resolution. So if you have purchased a 3.3-megapixel camera and you are taking pictures to share on the Web, you usually can change a setting in the camera to take a lower-resolution image. And, just in case you weren't already confused enough, you will find that the settings in the camera seldom mention megapixels and instead list the resolutions by a name or group of letters.

Important

MACRO FEATURE

If the camera has a *macro* feature, this setting allows you to get within centimeters of the document or object you wish to take a picture of. It helps the camera to focus better at such a short distance, retaining the field of depth among other things.

WHAT'S THE BEST FILE FORMAT?

Almost all of the digital cameras available today default to saving the pictures in a JPEG format. JPEG is the acronym for *Joint Photographic Experts Group*, and the format is named after the group that established the standard image compression algorithm. It is through the math that the file format achieves such a high rate of compression, giving us a chance to save as many pictures as possible to a storage card. However, with compression comes loss of data, though it is usually not enough to affect the picture when you print it.

For those instances when you need a perfect picture, see if your camera will save a priceless image in either a TIFF or RAW format. TIFF stands for *Tagged Image File Format* and it is a high-quality image that can be viewed on both a Windows and a Mac system. TIFF files are often used in print work. RAW is not actually an acronym, but the format of the image, as in raw format, retaining all the image data, usually in the camera's native or proprietary format. Usually this means using the software that came with the camera to open and convert the files.

Both TIFF and RAW files have the potential to be huge in megabytes. The JPEG format is much smaller, as it already has been compressed. When sharing JPEG files via e-mail attachments, you will not be able to compress or "zip" them up any further. TIFF and RAW files can be compressed, but will still be rather large files.

Remember that in addition to the file format you are saving in—JPEG vs. TIFF—the resolution also affects the number of images that can be stored on the camera, either in the camera's internal storage or on a storage card. You will learn more about storage cards shortly.

Exposure Controls

Depending on the type of digital camera you are interested in, additional exposure controls may be available, including some manual controls that closely resemble high-end traditional 35mm cameras. Most of the cameras available in the point-and-click and intermediate categories have preset exposure settings. You may have a couple of choices for shooting pictures inside or outside, but beyond that the camera is probably relying on a full auto-exposure setting for the pictures you take.

As you get into the advanced consumer and higher-end categories, you begin to get more features found commonly on high-end 35mm traditional cameras. These may include the ability to under- or overexpose an image, aperture settings, and shutter speed control. **The lens opening (aperture) settings may be referred to as f-stops, and they control the size of the lens opening to help**

\di'fin\ *vb*

Definitions

get the best picture in varying levels of light. The shorter the shutter, the faster action shot you can take. After all, you never know when that tombstone might just up and take off. But seriously, exposure controls offer flexibility when you find yourself in the cemetery on a less-than-optimum day and it is the only day you have to take the pictures.

ALPHABET SOUP

ISO/ASA settings are used to define the amount of light film needs by identifying the film through film speed. Digital cameras have incorporated these settings because many people understand them from traditional film cameras. The smaller the ISO number, the more light is needed, but the better the quality of the resulting picture.

ISO is not an acronym, but comes from the International Organization for Standardization. This group sets the standards for each film speed so that photographers know what to expect from film of a given ISO number. It replaced the ASA standards, which came from the American Standards Association, now known as the American National Standards Institute.

Some digital cameras default to ISO 64, though you may have features in the camera that change this. Some feature-rich, intermediate or advanced digital cameras even have ISO settings that can go as high as ISO 400 film, a film speed designed for lower lighting levels.

One other exposure-control feature that should be mentioned is the ISO settings. Most digital cameras default to the equivalent of having ISO 100 or 200 film in a traditional camera. Like many of the other things we have discussed about scanners and cameras, the higher the ISO number the more sensitive the camera is, and the better the chance of capturing a good picture in low lighting. You probably remember seeing 35mm film with ISO ratings of 400, 800, or 1,000. But that doesn't mean you must have a digital camera that offers ISO settings. In most instances the default setting of the camera is more than sufficient for taking the types of pictures genealogists like best. In some instances the higher speed (ISO numbers) films lose some of the quality and contrast that we want. If you get a camera with which you can make changes to the ISO setting, you may want to experiment with the different settings on a single object to see if you notice any loss of quality.

Flash Options

All digital cameras come with some type of flash ability. The question then becomes: Is it enough for what you may want to do with the camera?

It is always helpful to have a camera that just knows when to use the flash.

But there are times when I want to be able to turn it off, perhaps because it is not going to affect what I am taking a picture of. A flash has a limited distance at which it is effective. So when looking for a digital camera I want one that offers an auto-on but that also has manual options. The good news is that most of the cameras in the point-and-click, intermediate, and advanced consumer categories offer that flash flexibility.

Viewfinder Options

Perhaps one of the most important things about the camera you are thinking about choosing is the type of a viewfinder it has and how well it works. A typical digital camera has an optical viewfinder, an LCD viewfinder, or perhaps both.

The optical viewfinder is a more traditional viewfinder. You will recognize it on any camera—that small rectangle somewhere at the top of the camera that you squint one eye through to frame your picture. For those who wear glasses, especially bi- or trifocals, it sometimes takes a lot of practice to become familiar enough at where to put the camera and where your eye needs to be to effectively and quickly look into the viewfinder and snap a picture.

Most digital cameras, primarily because of the menu options they display, have another viewfinder, the LCD (liquid crystal display) viewfinder. You could think of this as a small (approximately two-inch) monitor for your

---

THE WINDOWS TO THE SOUL?

They say that the eyes are the windows to the soul, and there are times when we are looking at photographs that we wonder if that is what we are seeing in the center of the eye. Actually what you are seeing is the result of the flash of a camera being too close to the lens, and as the flash goes off, it is reflected off of the individual's retina back to the camera, which then saves it forever on the film. I have always thought it left people with a haunting stare.

Present-day digital cameras, and many traditional cameras, have tried to reduce the effect of red-eye by sending some strobe-like pre-flashes to help constrict the pupil before the flash when the picture is actually taken. The smaller pupil cannot reflect as much of the flash, thus reducing the red-eye effect.

Ideally the best way to prevent red-eye is to use an accessory flash, but this option is usually limited to higher-end digital cameras that accept peripherals. By moving the flash away from the lens, the cause of red-eye is eliminated.

If you find that your pictures are showing red-eye, see if the camera has a red-eye reduction feature, but you may be able to solve the problem in editing. Many image-editing programs come with red-eye removal options.

Definitions

PARALLAX CORRECTION LINES

Parallax correction lines are the white lines you see when you look through the optical viewfinder. They help you to frame the picture accordingly so that you get everything into the picture that you intended.

camera. In addition to displaying and allowing you to set the options on your camera, it acts as a viewer to show you what the camera is seeing, and then as a display screen to play back the pictures you have taken. Because it shows you what the camera is seeing, if you have an item framed in the LCD viewer, you most likely have it framed for the picture as well. **While the LCD viewer is easy to see indoors, when you get into bright sunlight it fades considerably, making it next to impossible to tell whether or not you got a good picture.** The other downside to the LCD display is that it dramatically shortens the life of the batteries of the camera.

If the camera you decide to purchase offers both, then I would suggest using the LCD at times when lighting allows you to see it clearly and you need to get a quick shot, and reserving the optical viewfinder for those instances when you have more time to properly align the viewfinder.

The more you use your camera, the more you may discover little idiosyncrasies in how each viewer works. For instance, I have noticed when I use the optical viewfinder, because of its placement slightly above the lens of the camera, that I must pay close attention to the space I give to the top of the optical viewfinder's parallax correction lines to ensure that I have indeed gotten what I expected—in other words, so that I no longer chop off the top of Cousin Maggy's head. By the same token, I notice when I am using the LCD viewfinder that I must remember that it is sometimes a shade behind what is actually going on, especially if I am trying to take an action shot. Because of this delay, I sometimes overcompensate when I position the camera because the display has not actually caught up to my motion yet.

Storage Options

Like computers were supposed to usher us into the paperless society, digital cameras were supposed to give us a filmless one. Well, my office seems to have more paper now than it did before my computer, and if I am taking a long trip I make sure I have lots of "digital film." By digital film, I actually mean the different types of storage cards your camera uses when saving the pictures as you take them (see Figure 5-4 on page 63). There are times when the size of the digital film—such as a floppy disk or a CD-R disk—affects the overall size and basic dimensions of the camera. The type of storage card also may have a direct relationship to the speed of the camera as well.

While the storage media really won't affect your camera selection, provided it actually has a storage media ability, I always like to shop around and make sure I am getting the best options available. Usually the camera can take any capacity of the specified storage media. Most of the cards come in sizes of 8 megabytes (MB), 16 MB, 32 MB, 64 MB, 128 MB, 256 MB, and 512 MB. A couple offer even more space but, as you may have suspected, they also come with a higher price tag. Most of the cameras available today will take one or more of the following:

- CompactFlash—by far the most common storage device, so as new, larger capacities are released, they are often released on CompactFlash first.
- Microdrive—may be used in place of the CompactFlash because they are the same size, though they do tend to eat up the battery life pretty quickly.
- SD Cards—about half the size of the CompactFlash, and not as common, though I have seen some notebook computer systems that read SD Cards without a special card reader.
- SmartMedia—similar in shape to the CompactFlash, but thinner, this option is more common outside of the United States, particularly in Japan.
- Sony Memory Stick—a proprietary medium usable in many Sony devices, it is the size and shape of a small stick of gum.
- xD Card—the tiniest memory card I have seen yet, it was designed to minimize power consumption, an important trait when relying on batteries.
- CD-R/RW—found primarily in Sony cameras, the full-size writable compact disc requires a bigger camera.

Figure 5-4
Media cards come in many different shapes and storage abilities, but they are all relatively small. Beginning at the middle of the top line and moving clockwise, you see an SD Card (256 MB), a CompactFlash (256 MB), an xD Card (64 MB), and a Sony Memory Stick (64 MB).

Batteries

Digital cameras only work if they are able to turn on. Most of them use one or more batteries. Some of them are designed to recharge their batteries, while others can use any standard battery, allowing you flexibility of picking up a set when you need them or of buying the more expensive rechargeables.

Important

Internet Source

BATTERIES.COM

If you are in need of batteries and are tired of paying high prices, you may want to check out the savings at Batteries.com <www.batteries.com>.

By now it is possible that you have your eye set on a particular camera based on the other features discussed. **The battery type and number may decide which camera you choose.** I say that as someone who has used a number of different digital cameras with different batteries. The type of battery used can make you almost hate the camera.

When investigating any camera, find out the type of battery used and how many it requires. Some use standard AA batteries, while others use a more unique camera-specific battery, such as a 2CR5. Some cameras are designed to charge the batteries as you set the camera in a cradle, while others allow you to use an external charger.

I encourage you to get a camera that uses AA batteries. This usually gives you the most flexibility. On the fly you can use the traditional AA batteries, though the battery life will not be anywhere near that of some of the other types of AA batteries that are available on today's market. The specialized batteries, as in non-AA, are much harder to find. There were times when I would raid the local Wal-Mart before heading out on a trip to ensure that I had enough batteries to accomplish all that I wanted, especially if I was heading out of the country.

Currently batteries are found in one of two categories:

- One-Time Use
  - Alkaline—traditional batteries that we use in all manner of portable devices. The life of an alkaline is shorter than some of the other battery types mentioned.
  - Titanium—while still in the Alkaline class, Titanium batteries have an extended life. They are specifically designed for high-tech devices.
  - Lithium—also known as "photo batteries," lithium batteries offer even longer battery life than the titanium ones, and without some of limitations, like faster drain in colder weather.
- Rechargeable
  - NiCAD—Nickel Cadmium batteries are best known for their "memory." It is necessary to always fully discharge the battery before recharging—otherwise it will remember that it was 70 percent charged when plugged in, and the next time it will only charge to 70 percent.
  - NiMH—Nickel Metal Hydride batteries are a great advantage over the NiCAD. They have more current and no memory, allowing for better overall performance.

Rechargeables? Don't Forget to Plug 'Em In

When it comes to charging the rechargeable kind, if they are proprietary to your camera, then it is possible that you must have the camera either plugged in or cradled during the charging process. To me this means I cannot use the camera whenever I want to because it must also charge the batteries.

Tip

If your digital camera is using standard batteries, I suggest always having at least one complete set of one-time use batteries, preferably the lithium, so that if your rechargeables die, you can still take pictures.

If the camera uses a standard style of battery, such as the AA, then you may find that the charger is a stand-alone cradle or case into which you place the batteries when they need to be charged. My camera came with a special plug-in charging device that I place four batteries in at a time. I have two sets of rechargeables and at least one unopened set of lithium photo batteries whenever I head out on a trip. Then, as I use the rechargeables, I make it a point to charge the first set as soon as I can after it has run out.

GETTING THE MOST FROM YOUR BATTERIES

There are ways you can use your digital camera that will help to extend the life of the battery:

- Turn off the flash if it is not needed.

- Use the optical viewfinder and turn off the LCD viewfinder.

- If your storage choice is between CompactFlash and Microdrive, use the CompactFlash, because it is not as power intensive.

- If you have xD storage card ability, use that over any other, more power-intensive medium.

- Let the camera go to sleep when you are in between photos. You retain any customized settings, and it wakes up quicker than if you were to turn it on and off over and over again.

- Try to keep the camera and the batteries warm. Some batteries don't do well in the cold, thus shortening their life.

I have found that while I have a high-end digital camera, one in the advanced consumer class, which means lots of bells and whistles, it is also a great camera when it comes to battery life. I like to think that has something to do with the fact that I use fully charged NiMH batteries or the lithium photo batteries. I have been able to get three hundred pictures on a single set of batteries.

Ease of Use

All of the features—the viewfinder, the storage options, and the batteries—won't make a bit of difference if you find the camera too hard to use. Digital cameras take on some aspects of computers. Genealogists are generally far removed from computers beyond using genealogy programs. Many of the family historians I talk to are the first to admit that, knowing just the basics, they struggle with their computers. And since the digital camera is somewhat like a miniature computer, as we have seen with resolution and storage options, it would be understandable for you to be unsure of a camera at first.

So, when you have done all the research on the features of the camera, the next thing you want to do is to visit some stores and hold the cameras in your hand. See how they feel. See if you are comfortable with where the various buttons are located. Don't be shy about asking the salesperson if you can use the camera. Pay attention to the menus, and take pictures in the store. Do you find it easy to use, or are you frustrated? Did you get the picture you expected?

You also might want to think on it for a day or two. **Sometimes our worst purchases are impulse buys.** And when that purchase is an uncomfortable pair of shoes that didn't cost us much, then it isn't as big a deal. When it could cost seven hundred dollars, you don't want to regret the decision to purchase, especially if the store penalizes you with a restocking fee or won't allow you to return it at all. Look at many different cameras that have the features you find most important, and then decide which one is easiest for you to use. This is a truly personal decision. What you find easy, I might find most frustrating. I might love where the buttons are on a particular camera, or the feel of how it sits in my hand, and you may find that it is too heavy or awkward.

Reminder

I'VE GOT PICTURES, NOW WHAT DO I DO?

Another consideration with your camera is how you are going to get your pictures from your camera to your computer or printer. All of the cameras now come with a USB cable that can connect the camera to your computer. Your computer sees the camera through this cable as another drive, like your hard drive or CD-ROM. You can then use the special software that comes with the camera to move the pictures onto the computer, or you can copy (or cut) and paste them from the camera to the computer.

This is the method you will find described with almost every camera you purchase, and yet there are easier ways of moving the pictures, especially if you are not using the software that came with the camera. Also, these other methods will not drain the batteries of the camera as you are downloading the pictures onto the computer.

Definitions

USB

USB stands for *universal serial bus,* which offers a faster connection than standard parallel and serial ports for linking peripherals such as scanners and digital cameras to your computer. While not the fastest connection, it is the most common right now.

A CARD READER

Perhaps the most popular way of moving the images is to invest in a card reader. Most card readers connect to your computer through a USB cable.

PCMCIA CARDS

If you are using a notebook computer, you may want to look into getting a PCMCIA CompactFlash card adapter. I use mine all the time when transferring pictures from my camera to my notebook. The CompactFlash cards are inserted into the PCMCIA card, which then goes into a special slot on the notebook computer. My computer sees this as another drive and allows me to copy the pictures off of the CompactFlash card. Moving the pictures in this manner saves battery life, as my camera doesn't have to be connected to the computer when downloading the photo files.

The better card readers handle most of the different card formats that were discussed earlier. Some card readers are so small and light that you can take them on the road with you to dump pictures from the camera to your notebook. This should guarantee that you never run out of digital film on a research trip, even if you take pictures of every tombstone in the cemetery.

ENOUGH TALK—LET'S TAKE PICTURES

Now that you know all about the camera, it is time to have some fun by looking at how to take some great pictures. Digital cameras are great—if you don't like the picture when you take it, you can delete it and take another one. Taking a little time to see what your camera sees or learning how to make adjustments to the angle or view may mean you can take a few more new pictures on your research trip rather than having to retake a bunch.

SIX

Getting the Best Pictures Digitally

While I have confessed to being less than enamored with the printed results of digital cameras until recently, I must say I have always enjoyed the ability to instantly view the pictures I have taken. I like the idea of having a second chance to reshoot if the image displayed on the camera doesn't look good.

While the LCD display is not the best example of the picture, it usually allows me to determine whether or not a shot was bad enough that I should take another one. Sometimes, if I have enough digital storage space with me, I simply leave the questionable shot and take another. When I get back to a place where I can view my results better using a graphics program or viewer, then I evaluate the two and delete the one that is not as good.

GIVING A NEW PHOTOGRAPHER A CHANCE

The digital camera also has given me an opportunity to let one of my younger daughters become photographer for the day, which not only helped give us some time together, but also sparked her interest in genealogy. Since our trip to the cemetery in which she took the pictures, we have visited many other cemeteries and have taken a couple of trips to the library.

A couple of years ago, while my family was on vacation on our boat with a local cruise club, we docked in Key West for a few days. On this particular day, some of the boats were going out on one of many diving trips. When my daughter heard that I was going to the Key West Cemetery, she asked if she could come with me. I know she chose me because in her mind I was the lesser of two evils that day, as she had expressed that she was tired of diving in the salt water. I anticipated a twelve-year-old's attention span as we got to the cemetery and assumed she would be eager to leave shortly after we arrived.

Fortunately that was not the case. She was eager to see what I was looking for in the cemetery, as I had specific goals in mind for that visit, and she also took all of the pictures that day. We spent some time finding shaded places in the cemetery—which was a little difficult in the middle of July in Key West—to view the images as best we could as the day went on. At one point we did delete a couple and, as she likes to tell the world, I accidentally deleted one of the good ones, which left us retracing our steps to find the tombstone in question so we could take another picture.

Because we had the opportunity to view the pictures before leaving the cemetery, I felt I could let her take them. If a photo didn't look good, we would try again until we were both satisfied. As the day went on, her confidence with the camera grew, and there were less times where we had to delete and reshoot (see Figure 6-1 below).

Figure 6-1
Digital cameras give you the ability to preview images so that you are happy with what you have so you aren't frustrated when you get home.

I share this story to show you that the versatility of most digital cameras gives you a benefit that traditional cameras don't have—the chance to do it again while you still can. With this opportunity you need never go home and have a bad picture. However, there are some things you can do to take better pictures in the first place.

Important

Notes

LOCK YOUR FOCUS

Some cameras allow you to lock the focus. This is a great way to avoid the problem of someone's head tricking the camera's auto-focus. It allows you to pre-set the focus and then shoot pictures quickly, concentrating on your subject regardless of whether or not something else gets in the way. Your camera's manual should indicate if you have this option available and how to take advantage of it.

THE HAZE IS BEGINNING TO LIFT

Focus is seldom thought of anymore. **Many traditional cameras—and almost all digital cameras—have the capacity to auto-focus.** Be aware of the difference between auto-focus and "fixed-focus," which means there is no additional focus ability.

With digital cameras, a picture can turn out unclear because of a misunderstanding the camera used to take the picture. But first, a look at how the camera knows to focus.

Recently as I took a close-up picture, I noticed that a red "light" hit the object I was about to take a picture of before the camera actually made its adjustments. I have learned with my digital camera that the actual pressing of the shutter button is a two-step process. I press it halfway down and then the camera makes adjustments, which I can see if I am using the LCD display, and then I press it all the way down to take the actual picture. Seeing the red light reminded me that the camera is measuring the distance from the lens to the object about to be photographed. The camera does this by measuring the time it takes for that infrared light to be bounced off the object and returned. This allows the camera to adjust the focus to give me the best possible picture. Another method that some cameras use is sonar, which uses sound to bounce instead of light.

Now that I have described how this works, I bet you can see some potential focusing problems with the system. The biggest problem is when there is something between the camera and the subject you intended to be in focus. This happens to me all the time when I am taking pictures in a group setting, where I mean to be taking a picture of someone on a stage, perhaps, and instead the camera focuses on the back of the tall guy's head two rows in front of me. As a result the picture is out of focus for what I wanted, but is a really crisp image of every hair on the back of that man's head.

When it comes to taking pictures of tombstones, depending on how you angle the camera, you may find that the tombstone is out of focus but the weeds in front of it are perfectly clear. Similar problems may arise when you are taking candid photos during the family reunion, primarily because, if you spend the time needed to focus on the person you intended, they may notice you and spoil the candid nature of the shot or turn away completely.

Some of the focusing issues will resolve themselves as you become more familiar with your camera, including how quickly it can focus, and where you need to point it to get the correct subject in focus.

UP CLOSE AND PERSONAL

How often do we push a button on the camera to zoom in as close as possible without even giving a thought as to what it is doing? Any time you are really close to your desired focal point, the camera has to jump through hoops to give you a good picture. That is why in most cases there is a limit to how close you can get to anything before the image begins to blur.

Most people don't need to get as close to objects as genealogists do when trying to take pictures of documents, especially those that are too fragile to be photocopied. Other times we may want to take a picture of a unique piece of jewelry or some other item so we can share the image to ask for help in identifying the insignia, initials, or design. **Often such three-dimensional items are better reproduced as photographs than as scanned images.**

Getting that close may require a digital camera with a macro function, which should be turned on when you want to get within centimeters of an item. This feature is usually listed in any specification write-ups on a camera, and may require a menu option on the camera itself to activate it. Once the function is turned on, you will find that as you move the camera close to the item in question, it comes into focus. The macro function also may retain a good depth of field perspective, something that is lost when shooting photos up close without this feature.

The macro feature is a great way to preserve a letter by taking a picture, especially if the paper is already falling apart. A cousin may be more willing to let you take a picture of a fragile Bible page than he would be to let you make a photocopy.

Tip

Warning

I SEE THE LIGHT, AND IT'S BRIGHT

When you use the macro feature of your camera, you are placing the camera quite close to the object to be photographed. If the flash goes off, it will distort the image by showing part of it as quite bright, perhaps even washed-out. So it is a good idea to turn off the flash when using your macro feature.

IT'S ALL IN THE COMPOSITION

There will be times when you tear yourself away from your genealogical endeavors and want to take other, quality photos. After all, digital photography isn't just about genealogy—though I hope you will help me in not letting that get around much.

There are many things to consider when composing a picture. And because most of what genealogists typically shoot doesn't require good composition, it may take you longer to grasp it. Things to consider when composing a picture include:

- Balance.

- Visual interest in what the picture is about.

- Expressing a point of view through the picture.

- Using color, texture, and pattern to enhance the feel of your picture.

Check out the public library for books on photo composition. You also may want to read Steve Greenberg's *The Complete Idiot's Guide to Digital Photography* (Indianapolis: Alpha, 2003).

TO CENTER OR NOT TO CENTER

Go to any class on photo composition, and I anticipate that you will be encouraged to place the subject of your photo slightly off center. By off center, I mean both horizontally as well as vertically. This is to make the ultimate photo pleasing to the eye.

If you are taking a picture of your grandfather as he sits on a bench in the cemetery where the family is buried, then yes, by all means follow the suggestions of professional artistic photographers. You might even find that taking a picture of the entire cemetery and applying the off-center approach gives you a nicer view of the cemetery as a whole.

Figure 6-2
Don't forget to soak up the atmosphere when you are visiting the places where your ancestors lived, such as this wonderful street view of New Plymouth, Bahamas.

Don't limit your pictures to just what you find in the cemetery or to taking macro shots of delicate records. When you are walking around the town to get a feel for the place where your ancestor lived, take some pictures of the community and the historical homes that have survived (see Figure 6-2 above). This is another situation where applying a good approach to composition brings the image to life.

BUT WHAT ABOUT THE DOCUMENTS?

When it comes to snapping pictures of any document, centering it is the best approach. This helps to ensure that you get as much of the original in each photograph as possible, and it may make stitching the images together easier later on, even if the camera you bought wasn't designed to put photos together. You will find out more about this in chapter eight.

Tip

Centering the document in the viewfinder helps to ensure good coverage of the document. If it looks like it will take two pictures to get the full width or height, be sure when you are taking the pictures that you overlap them so that it is easier to put the pieces together later.

Remember when you are taking pictures of documents that you have a completely different focus, in regard to what you want in the frame and how it will look, than when you are taking landscapes, portrait shots, or even candid photos. Document photos need to be taken less for their artistically pleasing composition and more to ensure that the text of the document is readable. When you take photographs of documents, don't just assume it will be for your own use. Years from now you may decide to publish their contents, or you may want to share some of the information in the document on the Internet. Getting the best photographs guarantees that you will have those options.

A CEMETERY VISIT

Another place you will find yourself making great use of your digital camera is in the cemetery. With today's technology, researchers who in the past would only take pictures of their own ancestors' gravesites at a cemetery are now visiting any cemetery they can and then sharing the digital pictures online to help others find their ancestors' final resting places.

Tombstones often require unique angles to ensure that the inscription is

SHARING YOUR CEMETERY VISIT

Whenever you get a chance to visit a cemetery, take a few extra pictures while you are there. With digital film it is easy to do, and you never know who you may help.

There are two great places for sharing photos of tombstones via the Web. Both sites are free to the public, so you don't have to worry about someone making money off of your generosity. And both offer fields for you to supply additional information, if known, about the individual whose tombstone you are sharing.

Find-A-Grave <www.findagrave.com> started originally as a place for people to share photos of the tombstones they had for those who were rich, famous, infamous, or noteworthy. They since have opened a separate section for sharing tombstones of just our average ancestors.

Virtual Cemetery is housed at Genealogy.com <www.genealogy.com> in the community section. You also can get to it directly at <www.genealogy.com/vcem_welcome.html>. While Genealogy.com is a commercial site, the Virtual Cemetery is a free electronic memorial where you can share as well as search.

THE SUN IS TOO BRIGHT

Ever stand outside in the sun and shade your eyes? What happens? It is easier for you to see. Have you ever thought about shading the lens of your camera? You might want to. The camera will react in much the same way as your eyes do, and you might get a better picture.

readable. Unfortunately, many of the types of stone that were used in the past are proving unable to pass the test of time and are slowly eroding away, never to be read again. Shooting the stone from different angles takes advantage of shadows that may be playing on the stone, depending on what time of day it is and where the sun may be. There have been times when I took a photo at one angle and it was almost illegible, and yet by approaching the stone from the other side, the shadows brought out the letters.

Knowing where the sun is and how it is shining on the stone may help you in this respect. Photographers suggest having the sun behind you shining over your shoulder. But many times you will find that neither the sun nor the tombstone are willing to cooperate with this brilliant advice.

WHEN SHOULD YOU FLASH?

If you leave your camera's settings on automatic, the camera will decide when it needs to use the flash. Of course, there are times when I have disagreed with my camera on just when to use the flash. Other good reasons to check the photo in the LCD window before moving on are peace of mind that the picture is a keeper and to make sure the flash hasn't faded or bleached out the picture.

With digital cameras, you often have more than one type of flash available. You definitely should check online sites, reviews, and your manual to see if your camera offers any of these.

- Backlight—helps to overcome any extra-bright background behind your subject.
- Fill Flash—can be used to soften shadows as well as lighten those areas that are shadowed.
- Bounce Flash—keeps the flash from hitting the subject or object square; instead the light "bounces" off of a wall or other flat surface, still rendering a flash but softening it.
- Red-Eye Reduction—flashes in a strobe of sorts that adjusts the eyes so that when the picture is taken, the eyes do not appear on the picture with red spots in the center.

STEADY THERE

If you begin to experiment with some of the flash options on your camera, or if you master the art of changing the shutter speed, **you may find that you need to familiarize yourself with various tripods to help keep the camera steady as it takes each picture.** This is especially true if you slow down the shutter speed, which keeps the shutter open longer and can cause the picture to be ruined if the camera is moved.

Tripods come in all shapes and styles and, as you might have expected, all manners of price tags as well. When getting a stand-up tripod—the kind you can set on the floor and still have the camera at chest level—be sure that it is sturdy. You don't want the camera to fall over and go crashing to the floor. The better ones may have a Teflon coating on the legs to make them move more smoothly as you adjust them to get the best picture. You may find that getting more height in the legs or a tripod that folds up compactly for portability may increase the price.

GETTING THE MOST FROM YOUR FLASH

Because the flash is built into the camera and the auto-flash just knows when to go off, we sometimes ignore this valuable feature. However, if you put a little thought into the flash, you may find that you get better pictures.

- It is best to be ten to fifteen feet from your subject when using the flash. Too close and the subject is washed out. Too far and the flash is ineffectual.

- The flash has a limit as to how wide it reaches as well. Your best bet is to keep the subjects together, having the group no wider apart than six to eight feet.

- The flash should be higher than the lens. If you flip the camera to get a portrait shot rather than a landscape shot, remember to flip it so that the flash is still above the lens.

Tripods are also an excellent way to take pictures of documents. Depending on the settings you have to use to get a good photographic copy, you may need the steady, unmoving feature of a tripod.

In addition to the tall, free-standing tripod, you may want to investigate the price of smaller, table-top varieties. Using a smaller tripod is probably the best approach when taking pictures of documents.

REALLY GET TO KNOW YOUR CAMERA

Take it from someone who knows: The time to get to know your camera is not in the middle of the cemetery or while attending the family reunion. **The time to get to know your camera is well before you make any of these trips.** But I do understand how busy lives prevent us from doing everything we would like to before a research trip.

If you don't have the chance to really play with your camera before you head off for a vacation or research trip, then see if there are ways to play with it on the way. If you are flying, you will probably have some time to kill in the airport. Use that time to snap some pictures and investigate what some of the different

KNOW BEFORE YOU GO

More and more we are using our gadgets and gizmos in libraries and other repositories. Sometimes they are welcome; sometimes they are not. If you are planning a trip to a major library or repository, check to see if they have guidelines on their Web site (see Figure 6-3 on page 76). If they don't, you may want to take a few minutes and either e-mail them or, if you are visiting soon, give them a call. It's better to know before you go so you can pack accordingly.

settings mean, especially if you do not understand them as described in your camera's manual. If you feel funny about snapping pictures of total strangers in the airport, bring the manual along and get into some fascinating reading.

I am really only half-kidding about the fascinating reading, but regardless, it is still a good way to learn about your camera. And I can tell you that you would not be the only one. I have read camera manuals and scanner manuals, and I have seen others sitting in terminals doing the same thing. I just hope that the one guy I saw who appeared to be reading and rereading it was able to grasp everything it said.

Being a tactile person, I must read and touch at the same time. I prefer to try a few steps from the accompanying manual and then see what happens when I do those steps before I read on. That way I can compare the outcome I had with what the manual or review said should have happened.

YOU ARE NOT ALONE

Because we spend so much of our time sitting at a computer, hunching over a microfilm reader, or traipsing through cemeteries, it is easy to begin to believe that you are the only person interested in family history and, more

Figure 6-3
Some repositories, like the National Archives, are posting their policies for scanning and digitizing documents on the premises on their Web sites.

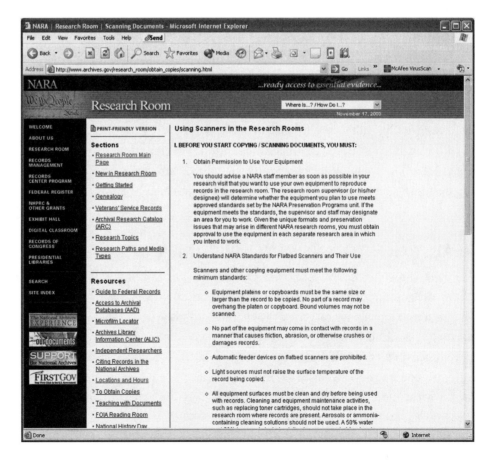

KNOW BEFORE YOU GO, PART II

If you are planning on using your digital camera to take pictures while reading microfilm at the library, know how to silence the camera before you go. Recently I spent a day listening to another researcher's camera beep as she took picture after picture of the images she was viewing. She didn't have her flash on, but the constant beeping as each picture was taken was an intrusion on myself and others as we tried to focus on our own research.

We all want to get as much research accomplished as possible when we are at the library, especially if we have had to travel some distance, such as a trip to the Family History Library. We need to be considerate of others as we are conducting our research.

See if your camera has an option for silencing all the beeps and other noises designed to make you feel more comfortable with a digital camera after having used a traditional camera. Be sure to turn off the sounds before taking pictures, especially if you are doing so at your reader surrounded by other researchers trying to do their own family history.

important, in digitizing it through things like digital cameras. Apply your excellent research abilities to find an online discussion group to aid you with your purchase and use of a digital camera.

The truth is, there are many different ways to get help with your camera. After you have read the manual—and some groups will make you read it for the first day if you haven't already done so—you can begin to branch out. Many photography classes are offered through local venues. They may not show you how to take a Pulitzer-winning picture, but they will explain why you repeatedly run into certain issues where your camera is concerned. The more you learn about your camera, the better your photos will be.

And let me assure you that, even if you do not see yourself as technologically-savvy, you can master the camera. In fact you may master it sooner than a savvier person because you are willing to acknowledge your limitations and seek help.

When I got my most recent digital camera, I fell in love with it immediately, read the manual, and began to experiment with it. This is how I found out that with my camera, the focusing takes place halfway through the pressing of the shutter. Now I know that if I need to quickly grab a particular shot, I have to already have the shutter button halfway down so the camera has focused and made appropriate changes. Recently my husband and I were at a function where it was easier for him to get out of the row to take some pictures, so I gave him the new camera and off he went.

When he returned, he complained about how terrible the new camera was. And as I looked at the pictures, I saw that we had many of the floor. He hadn't listened to my advice about how to work the shutter, and he repeatedly had pressed the button and then moved the camera so quickly that it hadn't had time to get the photo in place. To be fair, it was the first time he had used the camera, but because he is so comfortable, perhaps too comfortable, around electronics and other cameras, he elected to do it his way, even if that wasn't the best way. Getting to know your camera is the only way to improve your picture taking. Understanding how changing settings affects the overall quality of the picture eventually will begin to save you time. Don't be afraid to experiment with the camera. Remember you are using digital film. This is not etched for time and eternity. If you don't like the picture, all you have to do is erase it. In fact, learning how to erase single shots on your camera should be one of the first things you look up in the manual if it isn't easy to find on the camera.

TURN TO THE LIBRARY

As genealogists, the first place we turn to for our family history is the public library. In fact, some of us have been accused of living there. When it comes to other things, though, we don't always think of the library as a place to get answers. Shame on us.

Library/Archive Source

The library is a great place to turn for information on photography. Even if you are using a digital camera, many of the same theories apply, including composition, balance, lighting techniques, and the use of tripods. And the library has lots of books on how to take great photographs. There are also a few magazines for shutterbugs, and public libraries with large magazine collections will have some of them as well.

There are a few things that are different about digital cameras, but some newer books and magazines address these issues. Earlier I mentioned *The Complete Idiot's Guide to Digital Photography*, but you also may want to look for David B. Busch's *Digital Photography All-in-One Desk Reference for Dummies*. This seven-books-in-one is a great way to learn how to take good pictures with your digital camera and how to work with the images once you have them.

Internet Source

eDIGITALPHOTO

A magazine designed just for digital photography is *eDigitalPhoto*. You can find out more about the subjects covered in this magazine by visiting their Web site at <www.edigitalphoto .com>.

ROAD TRIP

Once you have your digital camera, you may be itching to head out on a road trip to take pictures of the ancestral homestead or the family plot in the county cemetery. Before you jump in your car or hop a plane, there are a few things that you should keep in mind, both in what you should bring and how you should expect to use it. So let's get you outfitted in true road warrior style.

SEVEN

The Imaging Road Warrior

A s I look at my address book, I realize that with the exception of my husband and children, my parents-in-law, and my own mother, all the rest of my family members are scattered across the United States. Even the places where my ancestors settled and raised their families are now far away from where I presently live. While there are libraries that bring some of the records to me, there are times when I must—okay, lets be honest, I *want* to—go to visit the counties of my ancestors. And then there are the times when a cousin has the family Bible or other personal items that I would like to have pictures of.

Traveling has become a way of life for many of us, and I marvel at the number of people who travel by air every time I get on the plane. The airport is always busy, and once in awhile I discover that one of my traveling companions is also into genealogy.

However, there is a difference between visiting a library—where I anticipate having photocopy machines and microfilm printers—and visiting the county where my ancestors settled for hundreds of years. There are times when I find that, through work or trips with the family, I also have opportunities to indulge my genealogy addiction. I long ago came to the realization that it really doesn't matter whose ancestors I am looking for, or whether or not a particular person is buried in the cemetery I'm visiting. I just enjoy the research and the reflection when I wander in the cemetery looking at people's final resting places and silently hoping they are not forgotten.

Thanks to genealogy, they never really are. And through the great cameras and other electronic toys that we have available now and that continue to improve, we may be able to help someone else with his genealogy or to help preserve tombstones or other edifices before they disappear completely.

THE TIMELESS TRAVELER

Before technology, traveling to visit a cousin or family homestead meant taking lots of paper and pencils and hoping I didn't get writers cramp if my hosts were in a particularly chatty mood. It meant spending hours in the cemetery transcribing the inscriptions of tombstones and, in my case, cursing the fact that I can't draw very well. It meant that so many of the elaborate insignias or other pictures on the tombstones were often lost, unless I could take a tombstone rubbing. Convincing my husband that I would just be another minute was easier when I was jotting names and dates in my notebook than when I was attaching a paper to the tombstone and getting out the rubbing crayons.

Before technology, we took pictures of houses, parks, tombstones, and family mementos with traditional cameras, counting every frame we snapped off to ensure that we had enough film to last the trip. We also worried about being able to afford to get them all processed, since few of us had dark rooms in our homes.

Genealogy was for many of us a personal adventure, and we gathered images and other things exclusive to our ancestors. Of course, technology has a way of making the world smaller, and—beyond e-mail and other subjects most people think of in this regard—digital cameras and scanners have contributed to the ease of sharing information. I am thrilled when people share scanned images of records they have located, saving me the time and trouble of requesting the same record. And from a record-preservation point of view, when a person shares a digitized image of a record she already requested, that record doesn't have to be removed from the book another time and photocopied.

So what should the traveling genealogist take along on a road trip these days? And what considerations are there to keep in mind about the gadgets making the trip and about what the traveler may experience?

ON THE ROAD AGAIN

My family has become quite mobile over the last few years. It helps that the children are no longer small children, but teenagers. This makes traveling with them easier and gives a flexibility to what we do that wasn't there before. It also means that obsessed genealogist Mom here gets to spend a few more hours doing genealogy than she used to when traveling.

Up until recently that meant taking a camera with me and hoping that I would get the chance to shoot at least a roll of film in a cemetery. Now it means taking a few more things and not worrying about the number of pictures I take. And I think you might marvel at the fact that everything I take can fit in a single backpack.

Rhonda's Road Warrior Supply Kit contains the following goodies:

- Notebook computer with power cord and extra battery
- Digital camera
- Digital film (xD cards and CompactFlash)
- Two sets of rechargeable AA batteries
- Two sets of single-use AA photo batteries
- Battery recharger
- Pocket PC PDA with power cord
- Palm OS PDA with power cord
- Portable scanner
- 4″×6″ photo printer with power cord
- Package of photo paper
- One extra ink cartridge for the photo printer
- CompactFlash PCMCIA Card Adapter
- xD CompactFlash adapter
- GPS antenna
- Necessary USB cables to connect above-mentioned devices
- Small tripod for camera
- Three or four blank CD-R discs
- Cell phone
- Two reporter-size notebooks
- Assortment of pens and pencils

A NOTEBOOK OR A DESKTOP?

If you are in the market for a new computer system, you may want to consider purchasing a notebook computer instead of a desktop system. The latest notebooks are as powerful as some desktop systems. And the prices on notebooks have come down considerably as well. By purchasing a notebook you can take your genealogy with you at any time, giving you a great deal of freedom: You can go off to research your family history without needing to print a book to ensure you have enough information with you.

Many notebook computers also offer an accessory that lets you use a regular monitor and keyboard when you are at home and then unplug the notebook when it is time to hit the road again. Such accessories, or port replicators, are designed to keep you from having to constantly attach and detach the cables for the monitor, printer, keyboard, and mouse.

The combination of a notebook and a port replicator offers the best of both worlds, as your computer easily goes from home office to road warrior.

I almost can see the look of horror on your face as you wonder how all of that can fit into a backpack. Well first, let me say that the backpack in question is designed for carrying a notebook computer, so there are perhaps some pockets that may not be in a standard backpack, making it easier for me to not only pack all of that but get to it all easily (see Figure 7-1 below).

Figure 7-1
With lots of pockets and space, this backpack carries everything I might need while on the road researching.

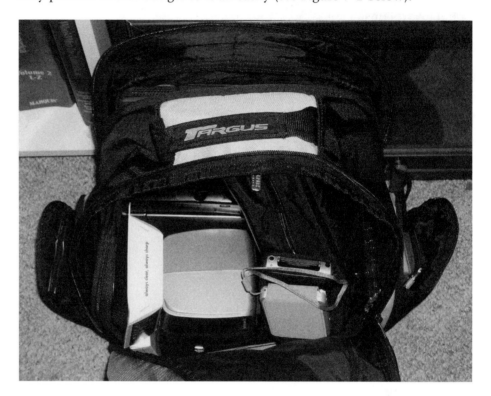

Also let me point out that most of these things are small and intended to travel. The heaviest item that gets packed is the notebook, which is about seven pounds. I suppose I could look into getting a smaller one, but given that I travel so much of the time and practically live on the notebook I have elected to get one that offers me the power of a desktop that I can take on the road.

The next two items that take up the most space, just by their block shape, would be the digital camera, because of the bag it sits in, and the photo printer. Most everything else is small or lightweight or can be combined with other things into a single bag.

I won't kid you, it isn't the world's lightest backpack, but I feel better knowing that I have everything I might need no matter what the trip involves. There are also times when I may pack most of this in a small wheeled bag or split the weight between the backpack I wear and the small backpack on wheels I purchased a couple years back. Deciding how many bags to take often depends on why I am going in the first place, and where I will be staying while I am there. If the trip is on the boat then space is an issue, so I take the technology bag and a bag for my clothes along with other essentials. If the trip is to a hotel and I have lots of space, then I usually spread it out through two bags, since I can take two carry-on items on the plane with me.

And while I am on the subject, **pay close attention to the type of plane you will be traveling on.** The commuter size jets have "little tiny overhead compartments," to quote a friend of mine. In fact, a recent trip to lecture had me scrambling to see if I could get my carry-on items stowed. I didn't have my road warrior supply kit, as I was flying in on a Friday, lecturing all day Saturday, and flying home Sunday. No time for play. However, on the last plane of the journey I was met with one of the smallest overhead compartments I have ever seen. In addition to having the computer and my small scanner, which goes everywhere with me, I also had my wheeled backpack filled with my projector, a small fold-up table, and the cords and peripherals. I thought I was going to be forced to check one of the bags. On the way home from that trip I repacked everything, sending the wheeled backpack as checked luggage filled with everything unbreakable and unessential for the trip home. But it was a close call and one that I should have known better about, given the many different planes I have been on.

Tip

WE NEED TO SEARCH YOUR CARRY-ON

In the last few years traveling by plane has seen some major changes. We must now remove our computers from carry-on bags so that they can be scanned separately. We often must remove our shoes, and those watching the X-rays of our bags are paying closer attention. As a result there are times when my bag of electronics has required a closer inspection. I completely understand this and appreciate their thoroughness. I can only imagine what the scanner and all the various plugs look like as they are staring at it on the security monitor. So if you become a road warrior, be prepared by adding some time to travel plans to account for possible additional searching of your carry-on bags.

I also take advantage of my travel time during airplane trips, working on the computer or going over my schedule on the PDA. As a result, when I book my flight I make it a point to not end up in a bulkhead seat. Bulkhead seats may offer more room, but they also mean that you must store all of your carry-on luggage in the overhead bins. This means you cannot launch into using the notebook as soon as the pilot lets you know you have passed ten thousand feet, but instead must wait until the seatbelt sign has been turned off.

NOTEBOOK AND SCANNER

A number of scanners are slim enough to be considered travel-worthy. The problem with most of them is that they require power. That power usually comes in the form of a power cord that you have to plug in—however, there are now a few that get their power through the USB connection to the notebook. Then all you have to do is connect the scanner to the notebook computer, and you are all set and can scan up a storm.

Some libraries are catering to these needs. The Family History Library in Salt Lake City, Utah, for instance, offers plugs at the microfilm cubbies or cubicles, allowing visitors to use their computers while working in the microfilm. Even the tables on each floor are wired for power, and these tables also include metal rings to use when securing your notebook with one of the commercially available security cables that work with most notebooks designed in the last five to seven years. With power and security, you can feel comfortable working with the books.

NOTEBOOK SECURITY

As a road warrior, you want to protect your notebook without feeling that you have to carry it with you all over the library. Security cables are one way to protect it. Most have six feet of galvanized steel cable that has a loop on one end and either a combination or key lock on the other. The lock is inserted into the Kensington Security Slot that has been a standard slot on most notebooks for the past seven years or so. Companies such as Targus, Kensington, APC, and Fellowes all offer a number of different security cables which can be found at computer stores, office supply stores, and elsewhere.

Family members are usually understanding about the need for power, especially if you're saving them the trouble of photocopying and mailing the Bible pages you're scanning. But finding convenient power near the table you may be using may not always be an option, so you may want to bring an extension cord or powerstrip.

Idea Generator

I also offer to burn a CD of the images I have scanned so that family members can have a copy of the photos, newspaper clippings, Bible pages, and anything else I've digitized. That way they, too, have the images in a digitized format for sharing.

Choosing a scanner based on its travel-compatibility limits the ones you can choose from. Thin flatbed scanners are the easiest to travel with: Just slip the scanner into the backpack so that it rests up against the sleeve. This keeps it from moving around and protects it some. If it has a viewable scan area and the clear glass is exposed, you may want to get a slipcase to put it in to protect the glass from getting scratched.

The scanner is a good option when visiting a cousin or other family member specifically to digitize photographs, deeds, letters, other family papers, newspaper clippings, and anything else that can easily be laid flat on the glass bed of the scanner.

Warning

There are portable sheetfed scanners, but I honestly don't recommend these for genealogy. They are great for business meetings where all that needs to be scanned is a contract or other contemporary printed material. Genealogists, on the other hand, are entrusting you to digitize their family heirloom documents and old pictures. Sheetfed scanners can be tough on these and, of course, are impossible to use with tintypes and daguerreotypes.

SCANNER IN THE ARCHIVES?

Never assume that you will be allowed to use your scanner in the library or archives. It is best to call ahead to find out what their policy is. I would suggest calling each time you go; policies change and you always want to be prepared.

SCANNER ON THE GO

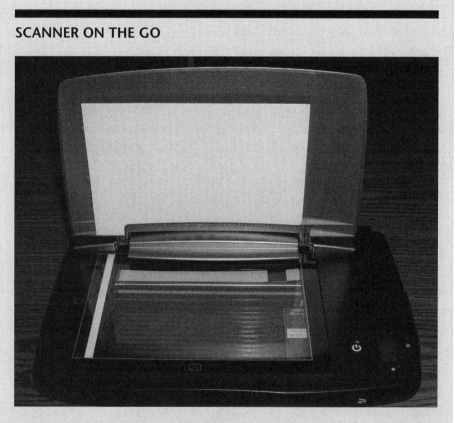

The PhotoSmart 1200 scanner by Hewlett-Packard is truly the scanner on the go. It was designed to run on batteries and save images (up to 4" × 6") to either SD or Compact Flash cards. This little marvel is just what the genealogist ordered. Take it everywhere; it offers three resolutions—300, 600, and 1,200 DPI—and an option that lets you mark a photo for printing. Even better, the top comes off, allowing you to flip it over to scan those photos or other items that may be glued into a scrapbook or other photo album. Inexpensive, this little dynamo was designed with the traveling genealogist in mind.

I also don't recommend the handheld scanners, because it is next to impossible to get a constant scan from human motion. We are just not as steady as a machine is. So this leaves the thin flatbeds. They are light and are getting smaller and smaller, so you do have choices. And you don't have to sacrifice resolution to get a lightweight model.

SMILE—PICTURES ARE ON CANDID CAMERA

While I always take my scanner with me, there are times when the camera is a better option, especially when I am in a repository that doesn't allow scanning. Always remember to check the rules of the repository before bringing any of your gadgets with you. Digital cameras can be used to take pictures from microfilm, microfiche, books, newspapers, photographs, and more. The key is to turn on the macro feature in the camera.

If you are in a library or archive that does allow photo-taking, you need to turn off the flash. Flash pictures are disturbing to those around you and could result in someone complaining about what you are doing.

In addition to the camera, don't forget the tripod. I have a small table-top one that I take with me when I am going to be taking pictures of photographs. This allows me to lay the photo down on the table and then make the appropriate camera settings. When I click the shutter button the camera doesn't move, and as such I get a better quality picture. I have seen some people at the Family History Library using a traditional floor style tripod when taking pictures of the microfilm or microfiche.

CAN YOU REALLY TAKE PICTURES OF MICROFILM?

A lot depends on the quality of the microfilm records, but in many cases you can. I know that some researchers use it to gather images of records on ancestors they aren't quite sure are related. They hate to make photocopies of the pages, but they also know it may be some time before they can get back to that repository. So, they take pictures of the records so they can review them at home to see if they do make a connection.

In the past this was a hit-or-miss approach. Today's cameras, though, are more sensitive, with higher pixel counts and more features. All of this combined means that you have a better chance of getting a useable image of what you were viewing on the microfilm.

JUST WHAT HAVE YOU DONE?

Too many genealogists avoid keeping research journals. Family historians dismiss the journal, scoffing that they can remember the research they have done. While this may be true when you are just beginning to research your family tree, I know from experience that after a few years it is easy to forget if you looked in a particular county for the family or if you checked the probate records for a specific surname. Research journals are not hard to keep. You can purchase a printed one, create one in your word processing program, or download one—there are a few places online where you can find them.

Important

For More Info

MICROFILM

Using your camera for microfilm means keeping a steady hand and not using the flash. A good tripod that allows you to position the camera at the same angle as the microfilm reader may give you a better picture, with everything in focus.

RESEARCH JOURNALS

It's always important to remember where we have been in our research. Keeping a research journal means keeping a list of all the sources you have used in a given research problem, not just of those that you find information in. Knowing which ones didn't yield anything is almost more important, because you have nothing tangible in your files to remind you of the negative research without the research journal. A great research journal can be found at the FamilySearch Web site <www.familysearch.org> by clicking first on the "Search" tab and then on the "Research Helps" link. Click on the "R" link, and you will find a PDF file of a research log in the list that you can download and print. You also can create your own using a word processing, spreadsheet, or database program.

While I use my research journal to keep track of the records I check and the results of my actual research, I also like to keep a trip journal for those times when the research or my activities are perhaps more vague. Often I am just scanning pictures or visiting cemeteries to preserve the records. But once in a while I learn something unique about a family in the cemetery, or I get the opportunity to meet a fellow researcher during the trip. These are all things that I will forget as time goes on if I don't record my thoughts about them as soon as possible.

Using a word processing program on your notebook computer is one way to record your thoughts and experiences of the trip. It doesn't have to be limited to what you did genealogically. Whenever my family goes on a trip I use my journal software to record all sorts of things about the weather, the traveling, and what we did. I often have notes about the facilities of the marinas we stayed at or the hotels we were in. This helps me later when picking hotels for future research trips. If a chain I have stayed at in the past is available and reasonably priced, I may pick it over other hotels because of my notes in the trip journal (see Figure 7-3 on page 88).

Tip

WHO IS WHO?

Another way to use a research journal is to record names when digitizing photographs. This is especially important if you do not recognize people in the photos but the person who owns the original pictures does. The easiest way to do this is to number each picture sequentially and then name the individuals from left to right.

I also make notes in parenthesis by the names when stories are shared about the people in the picture. I wish my memory was perfect, but usually

Figure 7-3
Keeping a journal of your research trip may refresh your
memory when working with
the images you captured.
Journal programs, such as
The Journal by David Michael,
are great ways to record your
thoughts and experiences.

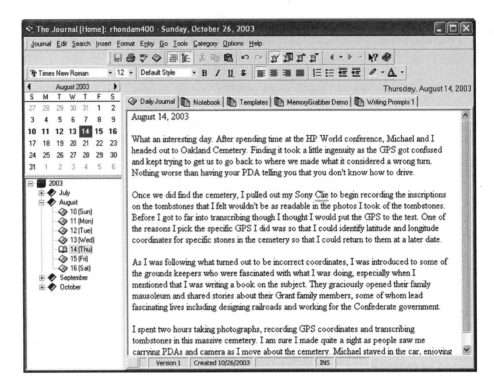

I need some reminders, and I prefer to keep electronic research journals because I can type a lot faster than I can write with a pen or pencil. And I
usually find, when scanning the photographs, that while the photo is scanning
I can be entering this information into my research journal so I don't feel
that I am wasting any time.

If you are scanning photos or other items at a family member's home, don't
forget about the person you are with. It is easy to get caught up in all the
gadgets and gizmos and forget that there is a human there with you. Make
an effort to look at the person and carry on a conversation while recording
the information they are sharing with you.

I DON'T HAVE A NOTEBOOK COMPUTER

If you don't have a notebook computer and are using a digital camera to
scan images, and if you don't want to take the time to write the information
longhand in a traditional journal, then you may want to bring along a tape
recorder to tape the conversation. That way you at least have the names of
the people and can hopefully put them with the pictures once you get home.
Keep in mind that some people feel uncomfortable around a tape recorder,
and this may hamper their conversation.

Don't hide the recorder though. Different states have different laws about
letting people know when they are being recorded. If you don't let the cousin

---

JOURNALS KEEP US IN TUNE

A journal is a great way to show how we have grown in the many different aspects of our life. Some people prefer to keep their journal by hand, while others find they are more consistent if they use a software program. Here are a few popular journal writing software products:

- eJournal <www.jorizon.com>

- LifeJournal <www.lifejournal.com>

- Alpha Journal <www.alpharealms.com/journal>

- The Journal, with Memorygrabber <www.familyhistoryproducts.com>

---

or other individuals know that they are being recorded, and it later comes out, you could find yourself in trouble.

NO POWER? NO GOOD

One of the most important things to remember before heading out on a research trip is that power is essential for most of the items in the road warrior kit. The only time I have forgotten a critical power cord was when I was flying to the Federation of Genealogical Societies' annual conference in 2001 in Quad-Cities. As I took off early on the morning of September 11th, all was well with the world. While in the air I realized I had forgotten to pack the power cord to my notebook computer. I figured that I would just call my husband when I landed and have him overnight it to me at the hotel. I wasn't lecturing until later in the week, and it would give me plenty of time to get the power cord and charge the computer.

Of course, that particular September 11 would forever change many things, and overnighting a power cord would not be an option. It would become an insignificant item when compared to all that the United States was going through at that point. But it did teach me a valuable lesson about planning ahead.

Now I double check everything and make it a point of going through a checklist of everything I need. I do pack my warrior kit consistently, which also helps to prevent me from forgetting something critical to the trip.

I make it a point to already have anything that uses batteries charged up at least a day before my trip. This allows me to pack most of the peripherals before the big crunch. The notebook and its power cord are two of the last things that I pack, because I am often using them right up until it is time to travel.

Reminder

I then make it a practice of charging everything each evening, whether I actually ran the batteries all the way down or not—with the exception of anything using NiCad batteries because of the memory issue. This guarantees that each morning as I head out for the next aspect of my research trip that I am prepared and will not be thwarted by my own devices; well, at least not because they lack power.

GOT THEM ON DISK—NOW WHAT?

While preservation is certainly an important aspect of digitizing records and pictures with scanners and digital cameras, it is not just for the sake of creating a digital counterpart. In many cases, the photos need to be edited to bring out the details so that individuals are easier to see or cracks in the picture can be fixed. Sometimes you can even lighten darkened corners of microfilm pages, making it possible to decipher previously unreadable text. To do any of this, though, requires image editing software and a little understanding of how it works.

EIGHT

An Introduction to Image Editing

I think one of the most important reasons people scan any of the photos they have, especially those in their personal collection, is so that they can edit them to make them easier to see, or to bring the people out of the shadows. Many of us also have older photos that may be fading or that have water damage, scratches, tears, or cracks in the picture. We would love to see the picture as it was originally, so we slap it onto the scanner. Now we have a digitized copy of the picture—complete with all of its imperfections.

So what does a genealogist do at this point? You grab the computer by the monitor, remind it that you are in charge, and begin to work with image-editing software to fix the problems and restore the picture. Of course, before you can become the master of the image-editing software, you first have to know just what it does and what key features you may need to look for in the software you decide to purchase.

The good news is that, when you purchased your scanner, you probably got at least a "lite" version of one of the image-editing programs that are currently available on the market. Such versions are not as full-featured, but they do introduce you to the interface, allowing you to decide if the program has a feel that you are comfortable with. I think the bad news in this scenario is that so many people struggle with these lite versions of image-editing software, which all too often results in nothing but frustration because of the program's limited abilities.

There are some key features that should be in any graphics program you select, and as the above statement implies, I do feel that if you are going to be editing your photos to restore them, then you need to go out and get the complete version of whatever image-editing package you settle on. These features are the ones that genealogists are most likely to need when trying to restore old family photographs.

WHY DO I HAVE TO DO ALL THE WORK?

Actually, you may not need to anymore. Scanners, such as the Epson Perfection 1670, are designed with those who don't know how to do color restoration in mind. The Epson Perfection 1670 is a photo scanner that offers one-touch color restoration, along with a built-in 35mm slide and filmstrip adapter. This scanner has the adapter built into the cover, which was discussed in chapter two. It also comes with Easy Photo Fix software that actually works with the scanner, so that by the time the photo is open on your computer, it already has begun to analyze the photo and offer suggestions for restoration before you do the final scan.

Once you have settled on a program, then you can begin to get detail-oriented with your photo restoration, which is something we will go into more detail about in chapter nine. Right now let's look at some of the terms that are common in all programs, and at some of the things that you are likely to want to do with your images. Then you will have a working knowledge of many of the terms and methods that will be applied in chapter nine.

WHAT EXACTLY CAN I DO?

While the image-editing software programs on the market are really amazing, and it would seem that you can do anything with the image you now have on your computer, let's take a moment to look at this more realistically.

Reminder

In truth, with patience, practice, imagination, and a good knowledge of the software package, almost anything can be fixed, enhanced, or altered. Of course, I have mentioned two things that genealogists don't like—patience and practice. Too often we don't take the time to learn the programs we have on our computers. But when it comes to fixing image imperfections, it often takes a light hand and quality time with your image program.

There are a few things that you simply can't do. If the image is really bad to begin with, perhaps totally out of focus, then there is little you can do to fix this problem. (But then, we never take out of focus pictures ourselves, so we've got nothing to worry about, right? Well, you may find a photo or two as you go from cousin to cousin that does have this problem.)

The good news is that most of the things that genealogists want to do can be accomplished with a little practice.

NEVER USE YOUR ORIGINAL

Since I have mentioned the "p" word—practice—let's start out with what I consider the biggest rule in working with graphics: Never work on your original image.

FIND HELP WITH YOUR IMAGE-EDITING SOFTWARE

There are books on most of the image-editing applications currently available. You should be able to find them at your local bookstore or through online bookstores like Amazon.com <www.amazon.com>.

Cohen, Sandee. *Macromedia Fireworks MX for Windows and Macintosh: Visual QuickStart Guide* (Berkeley: Peachpit Press, 2002)

Kay, David. *Paint Shop Pro 8 for Dummies* (New York: Wiley Publishing, Inc., 2003)

Kelby, Scott. *The Photoshop Book for Digital Photographers* (Indianapolis: New Riders, 2003)

Plotkin, David. *How to Do Everything with Microsoft Digital Image Pro 9* (New York: McGraw-Hill Osborne Media, 2003)

Rebenschied, Shane. *Photoshop Elements 2 Hands-on Training* (Berkeley: Peachpit Press, 2003)

Schwartz, Steve. *Microsoft Picture It! 7 for Windows* (Berkeley: Peachpit Press, 2003)

I seldom talk in absolutes, but this one is important. After opening an image in my image-editing program, the first thing I do is to save it in another folder so that any changes I make to it are not actually altering the original. There are a couple of reasons for this. The first reason that I work on a copy of the image is that if something goes horribly wrong when I am making edits and I mistakenly save the changes, I still have the original, which allows me to begin again. The second, for me, is that I often like to compare the before and after images so I can feel that sense of accomplishment. Too often when you work on an image for an extended period of time, working on just small portions of it, you forget that your hard work has made major improvements. Comparing the final edited version to its original counterpart shows you the results of the hard work you put into fixing it.

If you are just beginning to venture out into the marvelous world of retouching, that is the best reason I can think of for not working with your original image. Some of the images you may now have are not of photographs in your personal collection. Who knows when you will see again the original photograph that you used to create that image? If you make major changes to the image and then decide that it doesn't look good, you may be stuck with it.

WHERE DID YOU GET THAT COLOR?

A favorite picture I have of my mother was taken when she was about thirteen. I think what I like about it the most is that it is in color, and the color is vibrant even some fifty-seven years later. The original, though, does remind me of a coloring book, in that it appears that the color somehow was added

Figure 8-1
Graphics software allows you to create a more natural-looking photo.

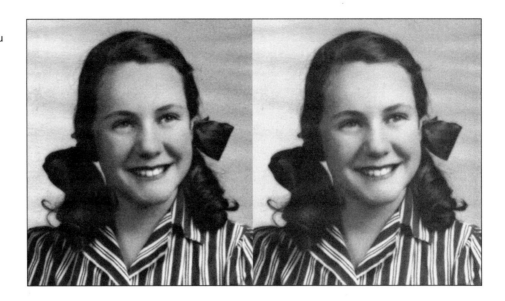

after the fact. I am sure this is not correct, but that is the impression I get whenever I look at this particular photo.

The picture has been scanned and added to my collection. The colors jump off the screen at me in a most unnatural way—it was one of the first pictures I attempted to make changes to. I had hopes of bringing a more natural skin tone to my mother's face, so I began to play around with the picture (see Figure 8-1 above).

It may take some time to figure out just which settings you need to adjust when making changes. Do you alter the hue/saturation, or do you change the color balance? Is it contrast that you need to change? **Of course, looking in the help file that is built into the program, visiting the product Web site for online assistance, or reading the manual may go a long way in answering these types of questions.** But then, we are genealogists, and I haven't met a genealogist yet who reads manuals before jumping into a new program. If we did we might save ourselves a lot of time and aggravation. These are a few of the terms that you need to become familiar with to work in image-editing software.

Reminder

- Hue/Saturation—offers a way to adjust the color itself, the amount of color, or the amount of white in the colors.
- Color balance—changes the overall mixture of the colors and is used for generalized color correction.
- Contrast—changes the overall tone of the image.

An understanding of the difference between hue and contrast makes selecting options and features in any image-editing program easier. But even if you have never had a reason to use such software before, as you experiment with the different settings, you will see the changes reflected on the image, and you will know if the selected feature has made the change you anticipated.

PALETTES AND PAINTBRUSHES

In keeping with the premise of working on a canvas with a picture, I suppose it was natural that so many of the commands and tools would be synonymous with the art terms. So I am sure you will not be surprised to find talk of palettes and paintbrushes.

In some image-editing programs, the palette is where you select the colors to edit your image. In other programs all of the miscellaneous tools are found on different palettes, each palette grouping like tools or options together. Selecting the correct tab for the palette that you want brings it to the front or expands it, offering you those tools to work with. This may include changing the colors and selecting a style to apply to the image, or the ability to select part of the image and crop everything else.

In the better image-editing programs, palettes can be opened or closed as needed and moved about within the program's window, so that you have access to as much room for editing the picture as may be needed—especially if the change you make requires you to zoom in and enlarge the view.

TOOLBARS AND MENUS

Like most programs, image-editing software is navigated by a number of toolbars and menus. While a few commands will be instantly recognizable—including the familiar copy, cut, and paste—many others are specific to editing photos and so have to do with color, brushes, patterns, and more.

The toolbar, a set of buttons, offers some of the more common tools used when working with images. These may include:

- Marquee tool—allows you to select a rectangular section of the image.
- Cropping tool—allows you to select a rectangular section of the image, and then eliminate everything outside of that rectangle.
- Lasso tool—offers a way of selecting a section of the photo based on curves and other lines, not limited other than that the start and finish points must touch.
- Healing brush—borrows pixels from elsewhere to heal or blend imperfections away.
- Clone stamp—borrows pixels from elsewhere in the picture for duplicating.
- Gradient tool—blends between multiple colors.

The more time you spend working in your program, the more familiar you will become with the tools and how each one works.

PICKING AN IMAGE-EDITING PROGRAM

I have often said that genealogists are more defensive of their favorite genealogy program than they are about their ancestors. As family historians begin

Tip

PREVIEW PROTECTS

Whenever you are making changes to an image, if there is a *preview* option, use it to see how it changes the image. This often makes it easier to undo the change if you decide you aren't happy with it.

Notes

to do more with their computers and use additional software, I see this trend is spreading, and I anticipate it will soon encompass image editors as genealogists become more familiar with them and what they can do. **Like genealogy programs, many different image-editing software packages are available, and different levels of features and price tags are associated with those packages.**

Some of the programs may offer a trial version. Even if you hadn't planned on using that particular program, since it has a trial version that you can download, why not try it out? It's a great way to evaluate whether or not the interface works for you, and whether or not you find making enhancements or changes to your digitized pictures easy. Some of the programs are easier to use than others, and some are missing tools that you might find essential in your editing.

IN A CLASS BY ITSELF

Before I get into some of the other programs and discuss some of the pros and cons of those programs in each level, there is a program that really is in a class by itself. Adobe Photoshop <www.adobe.com> is the Cadillac of image editors. This program has set the standard by which all other image-editing programs are measured. It has every conceivable option, offering you power at your fingertips when it comes to working with an old photo that needs restoration.

With that said, Adobe Photoshop comes with a price tag to match and a learning curve beyond what you may expect. Mastering the power of this program takes some patience and perhaps a how-to book or two. If you do get this program, though, you will find there isn't a graphics file format that you can't open, update, and save. In fact, there won't be much you can't do with your images.

POWER AND VERSATILITY

If you aren't ready to commit such a good chunk of your genealogy budget to a program reserved for editing photographs, though Adobe Photoshop can do much more, there are some lower priced and yet still quite powerful alternatives. Adobe Photoshop Elements <www.adobe.com> is one of these. Developed by the makers of the high-end Photoshop, Photoshop Elements gives you a lot of the power and function of the more expensive version, while combining that with some wizards and the QuickFix, a feature that makes the process of changing the image as simple as clicking a button. Another powerful program that falls into this category would be Jasc's Paint Shop Pro <www.jasc.com>. The user interface for Paint Shop Pro is a little more user-friendly, and it offers most of the same features as Adobe Photoshop Elements.

Macromedia's Fireworks <www.macromedia.com/software/fireworks> is

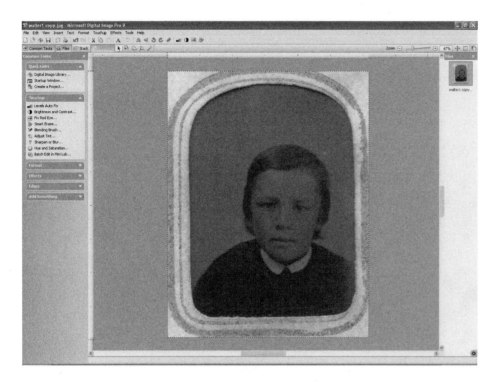

Figure 8-2
Microsoft's Digital Image Pro is easy to use and offers you a Smart Erase option to remove blemishes, such as the scratches shown here.

an excellent option for Web graphics. This makes sense given that Macromedia is well known for its Dreamweaver program, a great HTML editor that puts power at your fingertips. It is a little more expensive than the others in this category, though.

Microsoft's Digital Image Pro (see Figure 8-2 above), one of the programs found in Digital Image Suite <www.microsoft.com>, offers many nice features, including Smart Erase, a feature that genealogists really will appreciate because it is so easy. Smart Erase makes removing things a little easier by looking at the colors and patterns that are near the item you want to remove and using them to fill in the space. It does have limitations when the surrounding image doesn't have the necessary detail, and you may need to play a little to get good at selecting just the item you want to remove.

Reminder

CORELDRAW

If you have CorelDRAW <www.corel.com>, you have access to an image-editing program—Corel PhotoPaint.

GOT ANYTHING IN MY BUDGET?

Even some of those programs just mentioned may have too high a price tag for you. That's okay. There are some other programs that are much less expensive and still offer some interesting features.

One of the easiest to find is Picture It! Photo Premium by Microsoft <www .microsoft.com/products/imaging/products/pipinfo.asp> (see Figure 8-3 on page 98). This simple and too often overlooked program is a great entry-level image-editing option. Although it is not robust in its tools and functions, it does do all the important basics, including:

Figure 8-3
Microsoft's Picture It! is an inexpensive alternative for simple image editing.

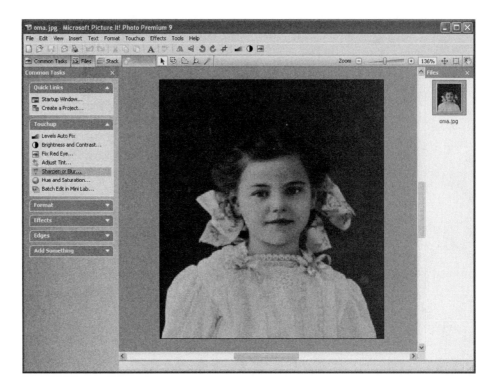

- Brightness and contrast
- Fixing red eye
- Adjusting tint
- Sharpening or blurring
- Adjusting hue and saturation
- Cropping
- Resizing

Picture It! uses simple menus, and much of what you want to use is found in expanding menus, similar to palettes in some of the other programs, along the left of the photo you are editing. And if you are using a copy of your image, then there is nothing to fear in trying any and all of the features to see how your various selections affect the image. You may be pleasantly surprised.

One of my favorite features of this particular program is its ability to print an index sheet. **An index sheet prints smaller versions—thumbnail-size—of each image file found in a particular folder on my computer.** This allows me to scan the thumbnails of the folder in question and open just the right picture in Picture It! without having to open every one to find the image I want. We will talk more about organizing your images in chapter thirteen and will discuss in detail how index sheets can be useful.

Another inexpensive, but good, image editor is Roxio's PhotoSuite <www.ro xio.com/en/products/photosuite/index.jhtml>. If you don't want to spend a lot of cash but still want some editing options, then Roxio's PhotoSuite is one you

Important

IMAGE-EDITING SOFTWARE FOR MACINTOSH

- Adobe Photoshop <www.adobe.com>

- Asiva Photo <www.asiva.com/photo.html>

- Cumulus <www.canto.com>

- Digital Darkroom <www.microfrontier.com/products/index.html>

- Enhance <www.microfrontier.com/products/index.html>

- Macromedia Fireworks <www.macromedia.com>

---

should put on your list to check out. One of the strengths of this program is that it is so easy to use, from the opening screen to the tools for making changes to your images. It offers much more, though, including the ability to create greeting cards and calendars. What a great approach—combining image editing and creative projects in one program. We will look at another Roxio product in chapter eleven, when we discuss sharing our pictures.

IS IT RESTORATION OR ALTERATION?

One fear that some genealogists have, and one that I feel is well-founded, is the concern that image editors offer the capability to not only restore a photograph, but also to make major changes to documents, which in essence gives the genealogist the ability to falsify information. We probably do not have the expertise that big Hollywood film editors do—who, for example, were able to insert actor Tom Hanks into archival, historic footage to make it look like he is meeting President John F. Kennedy in the movie "Forrest

Tip

TRY BEFORE YOU BUY

Many of the image-editing programs offer a trial download. This is true of Roxio's PhotoSuite. This allows you to try the program before you buy it so that you can get a feel for what the program can do.

COMPUTERS CAN'T BE BLAMED FOR CREATIVE GENEALOGIES

While we would like to blame computers for all the misinformation and "creative" genealogies that abound, the truth is that making things up when you can't find them is nothing new. In fact, Gustave Anjou (1863–1942) perpetrated genealogical fraud on many of his clients. He was not a genealogist, but a forger who often made up lineages for his clients when he couldn't find anything. After all, he was charging upwards of nine thousand dollars, so his clients always got a perfect pedigree. Many of the Anjou works are now found in the Family History Library—approximately one hundred and nine of them. So beware of anything by Gustave Anjou, as it may be a complete fabrication.

Gump"—but the potential is there. If a person is skilled enough with image-editing software it would be almost impossible for us to recognize the altered record, unless we make it a point to duplicate the research.

Restoring a photograph to its original beauty is a far cry from altering a document, to be sure. And most genealogists and family historians would never even think of making such alterations. However, when we correspond with individuals online, we don't really know who we are talking to or who else is reading our posts. It has been estimated that only about 10 percent of those reading a bulletin board or mailing list actually post to the same.

While it isn't an issue at the present, since most genealogists who have digitized a few records have not yet gone into editing them (beyond perhaps cropping excess on the edges), it is something that needs to be kept in mind.

When does it stop being restoration and become alteration?

Warning

Some people consider anything in black and white boring. There was a trend in the 1980s to take old black and white movies and "colorize" them. A number of classic films were altered in such a way. A scrapbooker may want to highlight something particular in a black and white picture—much as Steven Spielberg allowed the small child's coat to remain red in his movie *Schindler's List*—making it stand out or coordinating it with the colored paper on which the photo is placed. Such alterations should be relegated to scrapbooking, where the emphasis is on artistry rather than historical accuracy. Genealogists shouldn't consider the colorization of a black and white photo as falling under the auspices of "restoration."

There could be times when the genealogist considered it restoration and in fact it was an alteration. For instance, perhaps the genealogist is trying to enhance a tombstone that, through the ravages of weather and time, has become faint. The genealogist thinks he is doing other genealogists a favor by using his image-editing software to bring out the date, because he is sure of the date in question. But what if he is wrong about the date? How many people might be led astray by what started out as a restoration project and somewhere along the line crossed over into alteration?

Restoration should be limited to fixing those things on photos that have nothing to do with data. Fixing scratches and other markings on the photo so that the face of your great-grandmother reflects back at you without the horrible mark across her face is a great endeavor. Another example would be merging two or more images to show a complete view of the homestead, or combining four partial images to reconstruct a family portrait.

A STITCH IN TIME

This merging of multiple images to create a single larger image is sometimes referred to as *stitching* (see Figure 8-4 on page 101). In some instances the software that comes with the scanner or camera may be needed to put the images together. However, I have found that the more familiar you become with your image-editing program the more you will find you can do with it, including stitching.

One way that stitching is effective is when digitizing a document, such as a will or court record, from a microfilm with which you wish to zoom in on more than the scannable area allows. Instead of positioning the image in a portrait mode, which limits you in width, you might consider rotating it and enlarging it so that the scanner is actually scanning a landscape version of the top half of the page. Repeat this process for the bottom half of the page. Make sure you have a slight overlap between the two pages, as that makes it easier to put them together later.

Once you get home you can open each image in your editing software, then create a new document into which you place both of these pieces. The new document needs to be as long and wide as both pieces of the document put together. I usually look at the dimensions of each piece and then add the width of the two pieces to ensure that my new document will be large enough to accommodate both halves.

Ideally, you have enough overlap between the two images to look for the best break in the document to merge them so that it looks seamless when printed or viewed online. Once I have pinpointed the section where I am going to overlap the two—and I place the bottom half on top of the top half—then I reexamine the bottom half to see if I need to crop the top of it

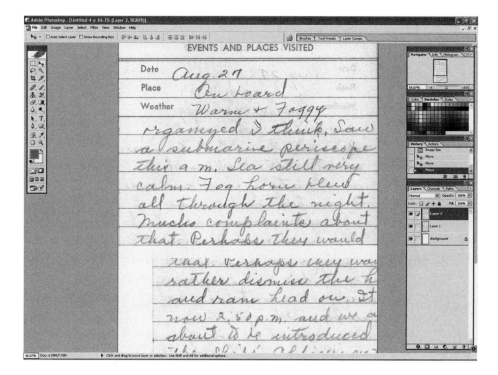

Figure 8-4
With Adobe Photoshop, you can stitch pieces together to make one image out of two or more.

> **FROM SCANNING TO STITCHING**
>
> Because I often must zoom in when stitching two sections of a document to-gether, I make it a rule of thumb to scan at a relatively high resolution. When I am scanning the images from microfilm at the Family History Library, I scan at 400 DPI. This is the maximum resolution their scanners offer, and it gives me a high enough resolution to make many different adjustments—including stitch-ing images together—once I get the images home.

to make a better fit. Seldom does it become necessary to stitch on the words with this method, as you can usually take advantage of the blank document background in between two lines of text, perhaps needing only to connect a tail or top of one or two letters at the most.

STITCHING BEFORE ENHANCING?

If the document I am stitching has some dark patches, I find it easier to edit these and other irregularities in the scanned image after I have stitched it together. This is not to say that it is the only way. You may prefer to make such adjustments before you put the two pieces together. This may mean doing more work, though, depending on where the edits need to be applied. If you need to adjust contrast or brightness and the sections in question happen to be where the overlap is, then you may want to put the two images together first, and then make the appropriate changes. If none of the changes would be affected by stitching the document back together again, then you may prefer to work with the smaller, separate images.

LET'S GET TO THE COSMETICS

Stitching two images together could be considered a cosmetic enhancement, but the true cosmetic tools that you may need to use on the images you are digitizing are almost as sharp as the scalpel used to give Aunt Daphne a face-lift. You can use these tools to give her photo a face-lift of sorts, too. If you get really good at restoring pictures, though, look out. Your family members may turn to you as "editor extraordinaire" before too long. Let's see just what power you have at your fingertips.

NINE

Working With Vintage Photos

I f you have photos in your genealogical collection, count yourself fortunate. Many researchers do not get into the research of their family tree until there is no one left who knows where the photos may be or who had them last. You can help share the photos you have in your collection by digitizing them. In the last chapter we talked about some of the software packages and the basic editing features you want to have in any package you settle on.

Now we are going to look at working with vintage photos. By vintage, we are largely referring to tintypes and daguerreotypes and how best to work with them. **It is more important that you preserve these, because there are seldom any copies lying around and certainly no negatives from which you could make another copy.** Once you've scanned these one-of-a-kind photographs you can share them with other family members, include them in a published book, post them to the Internet, and restore them if they have any marks, faded spots, scratches, or missing corners.

As we discuss working with vintage photos we will incorporate all of the methods of digitizing that we have talked about up to this point. Sometimes a scanner will be your best option, and other times you may need to take a digital photograph.

We also will discuss some of the unique restoration issues that may be relevant to older types of photographs.

Important

SCANNER VS. DIGITAL CAMERA

There are times when the scanner is not the optimum method of digitizing a vintage photo. The scanner's design or process may be too harsh on some particular vintage photos. The best rule of thumb is that when you are in doubt, you should use the digital camera.

Notes

CARTE DE VISTE

The *carte de viste* was quite popular in the mid 1800s. It allowed soldiers in the Civil War to carry photos of the family back home. The portraits were mounted on print paper and cut to the size of 4″ × 2½″. They were popular until replaced by tintypes. They were sometimes referred to as photographic "calling cards."

As we discussed in earlier chapters, the digital camera is best used in macro mode, and you will get better results if you use a tripod to keep the camera steady during the picture taking process. A small tabletop tripod is best, as it allows you to lay the photo on the table and keeps the camera relatively close, so that the macro mode is most effective.

DAGUERROTYPES AND TINTYPES

Daguerreotypes were invented in 1839 in France by Louis-Jacques Mande Daguerre, and their creation is considered the first photographic process. The process was the only one of its kind, and it involved a thin coating of highly polished silver on a copper support. Daguerreotypes are extremely fragile when removed from their glass cases. Once the plate was developed, a decorative mat, usually made of brass, was put over it to act as a spacer between the image and the glass plate that was put on top. This was then put into a case or frame made of brass to hold it all together. The daguerreotype can only survive if the case that protects it remains intact. If it looks like there is a bluish purple tint inside the brass mat, then the silver has begun to oxidize, and that means the seal has been broken on the case.

The *tintype* was a much sturdier photo, as it was made on a sheet of iron. The process was patented by Hamilton Smith in 1856. Tintypes and daguerreotypes are sometimes confused, because tintypes were sometimes placed in cases similar to those of daguerreotypes. But tintypes also were placed in cardboard frames, in jewelry, and in photo albums. Tintypes were common from 1856 until the early 1900s.

If your scanner has a document feeder that can be removed, you will want to do this, and replace the lid with the original one. The document feeder lid is too heavy for some of the items you might wish to scan, and this should be considered each time you want to use your scanner on vintage photographs and memorabilia.

Let's start by looking at some of the types of vintage photographs you may have in your collection. It will help you to understand a little about how they were made, and how the light and heat of the scanner may affect them.

SPECIAL CIRCUMSTANCES

Albumen prints were done primarily in the nineteenth century. They are photographs on paper that were coated with a mixture of hen's egg white (thus the name albumen) and sensitized silver nitrate. The *carte de viste* is an example of this type of print (see Figure 9-1 on page 105). These cards are sensitive to light, so make sure you keep them away from it. The best way to do this

\di'fin\ *vb*

Definitions

is to use a duplicate whenever possible. Based on scanner tests done by the Safeguarding European Photographic Images for Access (SEPIA), a project that focuses on preservation of photographic materials, the light emitted during a single scan should be safe. There is one caveat to this: albumen prints made before the 1860s. These salt prints, or calotypes, are much less tolerant to light exposure and should not be scanned; they should be photographed with a digital camera.

Definitions

CALOTYPE

A *calotype* is a wax paper negative from which a positive image can be made. While the image was inferior to that of the daguerreotype, the big advantage to the calotype was the ability to make multiple copies of the original.

Figure 9-1
Once this *carte de viste* is digitized, the tear can be fixed and the original protected from overhandling.

Gelatin-silver prints are the black and white prints that have been around for quite some time. Remember Eastman and his Kodak company? He worked with gelatin. The good news about these prints is that they are much less light-sensitive and can easily be scanned. Many such photographs, even your older ones from the late nineteenth century and early twentieth century, can be scanned without fear of causing any fading of the photo. The gelatin-silver emulsion was used until the 1950s, and probably makes up the bulk of your older photographic collection.

Ambrotype and *tintype* images are often discussed together because they are processed similarly. They are both collodion images—the difference is the ambrotype is on glass and the tintype is on metal. The good news with these images is that they are not predisposed to fading like the albumen prints are, provided they were not hand-colored. The hand-coloring, many suspect, is more fragile, because the photographers who added the coloring usually used watercolors and organic dyes that are subject to fading.

Figure 9-2
Daguerreotypes such as this one should be protected at all costs and are best scanned or captured using a digital camera. Never take the image out of its casing. Photo supplied by Maureen Taylor.

Definitions

COLLODION

Collodion was a liquid substance made by dissolving cellulose nitrate in ether and alcohol. Silver was then suspended in this liquid and placed on a glass or metal plate, depending on whether it was used in an ambrotype or a tintype.

Because of the metal in the tintypes, you may find that scanning them does alter the color of the digitized image. Some experts suggest scanning them in a grayscale mode for more detail. You may want to scan each one twice, once in color and once in grayscale, so you have both to work with.

Daguerreotypes are made by printing a silver image on a copper plate (see Figure 9-2 above). The image is then sealed in a glass packet. You can scan the daguerreotype without worrying about it fading, but when it comes to the glass packet, you may want to rethink the scanning approach and go with a digital camera. The lid of the flatbed scanner may be too heavy for the daguerreotype, and you wouldn't want to crack it when your goal was to preserve the picture.

Pannotypes are photographs on leather. Like the processes used to make ambrotypes and tintypes, the pannotype is made by applying a collodion emulsion to a dark surface such as leather or linen, resulting in a positive image. It would probably be better to take a digital picture of a pannoype than to place it on the scanner with the lid resting on it.

IS THE SCANNER'S LIGHT SAFE?

When we think of scanners we often think in terms of photocopiers, because they are the closest thing to scanners that we comprehend. And we associate heat with photocopiers, so we worry about light and heat on our pictures when we think of scanning. **Actually, the heat process in the photocopier has little to do with scanning the original and everything to do with adhering the toner to the page.**

Earlier I mentioned SEPIA <www.knaw.nl/ecpa/sepia>. It was this organization's working group that ran tests on the heat generated by the scanning head of flatbed scanners, and they discovered that it was not high enough to hurt these vintage photos. You can read their complete reports and other guidelines on their Web site.

When it comes to the light itself, you need to be more judicious in your use of the scanner. While some vintage photos can handle one or two passes by the scanner, none should be scanned repeatedly. Others shouldn't be exposed to the scanner at all.

One other aspect of the scanner's light that you may not have considered is the resolution you want from the scanner. The higher the resolution, the longer it takes for the pass across the photo. This increases the exposure of the photograph to the UV rays of the scanner head. Another consideration to the total exposure time is the number of passes that is necessary to scan the image. All scanners will do a preview pass and then, once you have made the appropriate settings and are ready to create the actual image, the scanner will do another pass. Some older scanners actually did up to three consecutive passes to compile the image in question. Avoid such prolonged exposure to the light of the scanner.

WORKING WITH THE IMAGE

Once you have digitized the photograph, either through scanning or by using a digital camera, then it comes time to embrace your image-editing software. Often times the vintage photos need more work to restore them. It may be that the image has faded some over the years, especially if you were unaware of the need to protect it from light. Or you may need to fix a scratch or tear in the photograph.

In addition to the basic editing tools you were introduced to in the previous chapter, when it comes to damaged photos you need more powerful editing tools, including:

- Cloning tool—allows you to borrow not only color but also textures from a section of the photo that is near the damaged area. It allows you to "copy" the texture and then "paste" it in the damaged area.

Important

Definitions

GRAYSCALE

Grayscale is a color scheme that relies on shades of gray from white to black. It is especially useful when digitizing black-and-white photos or other uncolored photographs, including tintypes.

- Lasso tool—allows you to select an area that is not square in shape. It gives you the ability to draw along an arm, a cloud, a piece of a tree, or some other odd-shaped component, which you can then copy and paste elsewhere.
- Sharpening—adds light and dark halos to colored edges—where the color changes—giving the illusion of the item being in sharper focus.
- Blurring—softens the focus of the background or the edges.

SELECTION TOOLS

Tip

Just as we don't look at our family tree as a single entity, we shouldn't look at a picture as a whole, but should instead work with it in stages. There are times when we need to make a change that should only affect part of the picture. Using one of the many selection tools, such as the lasso tool, means that you are telling your image-editor that you want to work with this isolated part of the photo. Whether you want to blur, copy, or sharpen, when you select just a piece of the image you have more control over the photo as a whole.

Many times, when working with digitized census records or other documents that are quite dark, I have found that using the brightness and contrast basic features on just a small piece of the document at a time produces a much clearer final image.

ZOOMING INTO THE SMALL PICTURE

One of the biggest tools at your disposal when working with your images is the zoom feature. Too often we begin editing the minute we first view the photograph on our screen at normal size. This makes changing the image much harder than it needs to be.

Instead of trying to work on the head of a pin, use the zoom feature to concentrate on the specific area of the photo that is damaged, viewing it in such a way that it is easier to identify where the damage truly is. This should make the editing process a little easier. And quite frankly, when you are dealing with damaged photos, the editing process is already difficult enough—no need to add to the problems.

IT DOESN'T NEED WORK

Not all of your vintage photos need to be edited; at least, not in regard to repairing a tear or getting rid of a scratch. But that isn't the only reason we digitize our photographs.

For years I have been the holder of the photographs for the maternal side of my family. And for years I have thought in terms of just my direct lineage, wishing I had better up-close pictures of more of my ancestors. Well, there is a limit to how many generations back I may be able to go, just because photos didn't exist before then, but **I didn't stop to think about the possibility of breaking down and enlarging the faces in the wonderful group pictures I had of my maternal grandmother and her siblings.** Perhaps it was because many of them are quite small, and as I looked at them I thought in terms of the family as a whole. I didn't stop to think about the true goldmine I had in my possession.

I have, at the very least, the ability to create headshots of many of the family members. The trick is in trying to isolate them from the photo without distorting their pictures. I think this is one of the reasons it took me so long to even realize it was a possibility.

The first thing I do when the photograph in question is of a lot of people—and, therefore, is full of small faces—is to scan the photograph at a higher resolution. This way, as I begin to select individual faces and work with them, I have the ability to enlarge each face somewhat without running the risk of distortion (see Figure 9-3 below, right).

Reminder

Figure 9-3
Family photos such as this one mean you have more pictures of relatives than you may have originally thought.

Figure 9-4
Once digitized, individual faces can be saved as new images for use in picture pedigree charts.

With the photo now digitized and in my image-editing software, I select each single face and create a stand-alone picture of each one. These pictures that I am creating are then incorporated into my genealogy program so that I can create picture pedigrees, or include the faces in my narrative style reports (see Figure 9-4 on above left).

While I don't have to zoom in quite as much when working on an image in this manner, it is much easier to select the face I want and copy it out of the original image when I have a slightly larger view on my screen. In fact, seldom do I actually work with the image in its printable size until it is time to print it.

For More Info

PHOTO PRESERVATION

A great book on photo pres-
ervation in general is Mau-
reen A. Taylor's *Preserving
Your Family Photographs:
How to Organize, Present,
and Restore Your Precious
Family Images* (Cincinnati:
Betterway Books, 2003).

Tip

THE PHOTOS ARE GLUED IN

I have four small photograph albums, the kind with black paper. They measure about eight inches wide by about five inches high. They are full of family
photos. My problem? The photos are glued onto the pages. And the pages,
because of where they were stored for so long, are not very strong. Flipping
them back and forth to place on a flatbed scanner is not good for the individual pages or for the binding of the books. Also, there are many pictures per
page—at least four, and sometimes more. This means that if I were to scan
each page, I would be subjecting all of the photos to multiple passes by the
light as I scanned each individual photo.

You might think that it would be easier to scan a page at a time and then
use my image-editing software to select each separate photo. Unfortunately,
the black paper has an adverse effect on the overall scan of the photos.

**Instead, I use my digital camera in its macro mode to digitize each of the photos
in the books.** With just a couple of exceptions, doing it this way means that
neither the books nor the pictures are subjected to any undue stress. There
are a couple of pages where the photos actually encroach into the binding—
these have required me to enlist the help of one of my children to hold back
the pages a little so I can take the digital picture (see Figure 9-5 below).

While I may still need to crop the images to focus on just one photograph,
this method is less harsh on the album and the photographs inside.

WHERE TO TURN FOR HELP

While many of the books mentioned earlier may give you enough insight
into your image-editor to effectively restore a photograph, I prefer the books
devoted exclusively to this subject. They often include exact steps for the very
problem I have with my photograph.

Figure 9-5
When photos can't be re-
moved from an album, a digital camera on macro mode
may be an option.

- King, Julie Adair. *Photo Retouching & Restoration for Dummies* (Indianapolis: Wiley Publishing, 2002)
- Busch, David D. *Digital Retouching and Compositing: Photographer's Guide* (Boston: Muska & Lipman, 2002)
- Ulrich, Laurie. *Restoration and Retouching With Photoshop Elements 2* (New York: Wiley Publishing, 2003)

SEEKING PROFESSIONALS

There will be times when, despite all of your best efforts, you may still not be able to get the image the way you would like it. In such cases, you may need to turn to a professional restoration company or a photography shop that specializes in photo restoration. Many of these businesses now give you a digitized image or images, usually on compact disc, in addition to your original and the restored version.

WHAT ABOUT PRESERVING MY VIDEOS?

Most of us seem to concentrate on our photographs, perhaps because we spend more time with them, but your computer also can be used to digitize and preserve your video- and audiotapes.

For More Info

PROFESSIONAL PHOTO RESTORATION

Just Black & White <www .maine.com/photos/Wel come.html> is a photo lab that specializes in photographic restoration and photo enhancements for genealogists. They specialize in copying all of the specialty vintage photo types, including salt and albumen prints, daguerreotypes, tintypes, ambrotypes, and others. Their Web site is also a great place to go to learn more about these specialty vintage photographs.

TEN

Digitizing Audio-
and Videotapes

W hen video recorders became popular, many of us took our existing 8mm home movies and had them put onto VHS tapes. That was probably some twenty years ago, and now you may be concerned about those VHS tapes and how much longer they will survive before they begin to degrade.

Audiotapes also have a nasty habit of degrading. And if you have recorded many family interviews, you certainly don't want to lose those, especially if they contain the voices of your relatives who have passed away. Those records may be the last tangible thing you have of those relatives, and you would hate to lose them.

Digitizing them through your computer may be an option. This does take a little more than just waking up one day and deciding to put your videotapes on the computer, but today's computers and software make it much easier than it once was.

To digitize either audio or video, there are some things you will need to get the 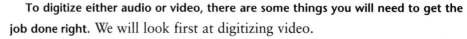 **job done right.** We will look first at digitizing video.

You need the following hardware and software:

- Video source—a VCR or camcorder, something to play the videos.
- Video capture device—newer computers may come with a video capture card, but you may need to purchase one if your computer doesn't have one.
- Hard drive space—a place on your computer's hard drive to store the file that is made as the videotape is being captured.
- Software—a program specially designed to capture, edit, and then burn the video onto a DVD.
- DVD burner—another item that may not have come with your computer, but that can be purchased.

- High-end computer—digitizing video is a computer-intensive activity that requires a computer that has the necessary graphics, sound, and speed to handle the process.

VIDEO SOURCE

Well, if you didn't already have the videotapes, then you wouldn't be reading this chapter. And if you have videotapes, then you have a VCR to play them. If the tapes in question are from your camcorder, then you have another means of playing them.

VIDEO CAPTURE DEVICE

The video capture card is an internal computer board that is installed on the motherboard of the computer. If you do not have one already, then you may want to do a little homework in this department. If you want the best possible duplicate of your videotapes, then you will not want to cut corners where any of the hardware is concerned. Fortunately, there are a number of good video capture cards available for under a hundred dollars.

When purchasing a video capture card, you need to keep in mind your video source. If you are using a VCR, then you need a video capture card that supports RCA-type cables. Also look to see if the card you are interested in has S-video cable support as well.

If both your video capture card and your VCR support S-video, the quality of the digitized video will be better. The S-video is used in place of the yellow jack of the RCA cable. Many camcorders also handle the S-video.

Important

GO DIGITAL—IT'S EASIER

Are you considering buying a new camcorder? You may want to look more closely at the digital camcorders. Their prices have come down considerably, and they are easier than ever to copy over to DVD. Unlike the analog tapes that have to be converted to a digital format, the digital camcorder tapes are copied rather than converted when you connect the camcorder to the computer to create a DVD.

Digital camcorders often come with a firewire cable, a much faster method of transferring data from one thing to another, in this case from the tape to the computer. Because the tape is already in digital format and because of the fast connection, the quality of the file that ultimately becomes the DVD is much better.

RCA CABLES

RCA is the acronym for Radio Corporation of America, but today it stands for the connector or cable that is used to connect the audio and video devices to a video adapter and sound card. There are three plugs on each side of the cable, and each has a corresponding color. The white and red plugs correspond to the left and right audio, respectively, for stereo sound. The yellow plug is for the video. Sometimes you will find a single cable with three plugs on each end. Other times you may find three separate cables. Neither is better than the other.

HARD DRIVE SPACE

The hard drive space may not sound like a big deal, but it is extremely important. When you begin the capture process, you need to estimate approximately four gigabytes of space for every twenty minutes of video you capture. Yes, you read that correctly—I said gigabytes. This is assuming you are capturing at high quality.

If your system and budget can handle it, you may want to look into getting another hard drive, one that you can dedicate to the capturing of your videos. Usually after you have captured and edited each video, you burn it to a DVD and then remove the raw footage from your computer—or at the very least, burn it off onto another DVD—freeing up the space again for the next video you want to digitize. But if you want to capture and edit an hour of tape, you can see that the file size is going to be huge, though in a moment we will look at whether or not to grab an entire full-length tape at one time.

\di'fin\ *vb*

Definitions

ANALOG VIDEO

Analog video refers to video that uses a system of unlimited variables when measuring the flow of data. There is no constant in the measurement as there is with digital. Consider that many digital devices—computers or binary systems in their own right—measure the signal as either off (Ø) or on (1), whereas the analog is not limited to that standard.

THE SPEED OF FIRE

If you have a digital camcorder, check to see if it has a FireWire port. FireWire is a high-speed cable connection, which may show up on your computer as an IEEE 1394 connection. It is used most often when a high-speed transfer is necessary, which is why you see it so frequently on digital camcorders. If your computer doesn't already have a FireWire port, you may want to invest in a card that goes into your computer with the FireWire port in it. But such an expense would not be warranted if you are not planning on creating many DVDs.

SOFTWARE

Part of the capturing process is done with the hardware; the tape's image is essentially played through the cables into the computer, where it is then saved to the hard drive. To do this, though, you must have software that actually tells the computer to capture the video in question. The software is one of your most important factors in this process. You want a software program that is easy to use, but that also offers you a good assortment of editing features.

Definitions

DIGITAL VIDEO SOFTWARE

- iMovie (Macintosh) <www.apple.com>

- Adobe Premier (Macintosh) <www.adobe.com>

- Avid Xpress DV (Macintosh) <www.avid.com>

- Final Cut Pro (Macintosh) <www.apple.com>

- Final Cut Express (Macintosh) <www.apple.com>

- Roxio VideoWave (Windows) <www.roxio.com>

- Pinnacle Studio (Windows) <www.pinnaclesys.com>

- DVD MovieFactory (Windows) <www.ulead.com>

- VideoStudio (Windows) <www.ulead.com>

- Visual Communicator (Windows) <www.seriousmagic.com>

VIDEO COMPRESSION

Video compression is a method of making the digital file created from the video smaller so that it is more manageable. This is done through the use of an algorithm. Video is often compressed and then decompressed as needed through a codec—which stands for compression/decompression. Just as we shrink a file using something like WinZip, a codec shrinks the video file, but then decompresses it only as needed. This is more efficient than WinZip, which completely decompresses the file regardless of need.

Like genealogy software, the interface of the various video capturing and editing software packages should factor into your decision, just as much as the features of the programs will. If the interface seems confusing or user-unfriendly, then you should consider another package (see Figure 10-2 on page 116).

The software should be able to handle the following:

- Capturing (through compression) and editing footage from 8mm and all analog VHS tapes and recorders.
- Capturing (through compression) and editing footage from digital camcorders.
- Ability to make DVDs from the footage captured (quality may vary depending on the original footage).
- Timeline features for frame-by-frame editing.
- Preview feature to see how the changes affect your captured footage.
- Ability to add effects to the output, such as fading in and out, and other transitions.
- Tutorials to teach you how to use the features of the program.

Figure 10-2
Video editing software, such as Roxio's DVD Builder, helps you convert analog video to image files you can then burn onto DVDs.

DVD BURNER

Once you are done capturing and editing the video, you should burn it to a disc, which can be done using either video CDs or DVDs. The DVD can handle more than the video CDs, which can store only about ten minutes of video. But they are a great option if you want to share just a small piece of video, because writable CDs are much cheaper than DVDs.

If you do not already have a DVD burner, you will find that they come in two forms: those that sit on your desk and those that can be installed inside your computer. If your computer has no more bays in which to place this drive, you may want to consider swapping the CD drive for the DVD one. The DVD drive can both read and burn your CDs as well as burn DVDs, so you will not lose any functionality by replacing a CD drive in this way.

DVD burners look identical to CD-ROM drives or CD burners. They are the same size as CD units, so you won't have any problems getting one in your system. If you are uncomfortable opening your computer's box, most computer stores will install such a device.

PUT THE PEDAL TO THE METAL

If you want to digitize video, then you need a computer that can handle it. We already have talked about the hard disk space needed, 4 gigabytes (GB) of space for twenty minutes of high-resolution video. It may be possible to

WHICH MODEL DO I CHOOSE?

There are many different DVD burners. Some of them sit inside your computer; others sit on your desk and are connected through USB cables. If you get one that uses USB, remember that your computer needs to support USB 2.0—the earlier USB 1.1 has too slow a data transfer rate, and the quality of the video file will not be good. (Remember that DVD burners simply make copies of video you've already converted to digital; if you want to capture video you also may need to get a video capture card.)

The following companies offer DVD burners:

- Hewlett-Packard <www.hp.com>

- I/O Magic <www.iomagic.com>

- Memorex <www.memorex.com>

- Pacific Digital <www.pacificdigital.com>

- Pioneer Electronics <www.pioneerelectronics.com>

- Sony <www.sony.com>

- TDK <www.tdk.com>

do what you want with a resolution that adds up to about 100 MB per minute, or 6 GB. Compression settings during the capturing process may get that slightly lower, but you can see that the file sizes are still monstrous.

When it comes to working with files of this magnitude, you need more than a lot of space on your hard drive. You need a powerful computer, as well. **The faster the CPU and the more RAM you have in your computer, the easier it is to work with those large files.**

Important

RAM AND CPU

RAM is the acronym for *random access memory*. Information can be read from and written to this type of memory by the computer. Information stored in RAM can be accessed randomly, which means the information can be retrieved more quickly, as opposed to, for example, trying to find the same thing on a tape, which must fast-forward or rewind to find the item wanted.

CPU is the acronym for *central processing unit* and is the brain of the computer. The CPU is quite small when you consider what it has to do, as it is just one small inch-and-a-half square chip inside the computer.

CHANGE THE WAY YOU THINK

Usually, when we copy or move something from one medium to another, we think in terms of entirety. That's fine if we are talking about our family history database or a digitized photograph, but when it comes to video that is not always possible.

Consider that the capturing of sixty minutes of video can equal at least 6 GB if not more. Now take that number and multiply it by the two to six hours of video you have on that tape. Immediately we can see that it isn't possible to duplicate the whole thing at once. And actually, when it comes to video, you usually don't need the whole thing, and seldom are you going to burn the whole thing. Usually, after capturing the video, you are going to go through it to edit out the mistakes—perhaps the dog jumped on you while you were shooting—and perhaps to tighten up the action. I know that many of the videos we have shot over the years of family gatherings have some dead time. When digitizing that videotape, you can get rid of any lulls like that during the editing phase.

Most video-editing software programs let you insert effects, such as fade-outs, just like you see on television shows, as they fade from one scene before jumping to a new one. You can use similar effects to make transitions in your own production so that the dead zone is not missed, nor does it feel like the video is jerky or jumpy from one scene to another.

Digitizing in this way usually means working with smaller pieces of original videotape, perhaps only ten or twenty minutes at a time. And as you work with this, editing out any dead time, you may discover that in the end the two hours of video tape is actually little more than an hour when you get just the shots

STREAMING VIDEO

Streaming video is a way to use the computer as just a conduit for converting the video from the camcorder or VCR directly onto a DVD. This means there is little or no editing involved. To stream video, you still need to have the heavy-duty connections that allow high transfer rates of data, and you still need the capture device and the DVD burner. What you don't need to do is sit there while it is transferring. When it starts, you need to pay attention to how many minutes can be put on the DVD, and then be sure that you are there as it nears the end so that you can stop capturing and stop the tape. This way you won't miss anything and can begin the next DVD at the point where the last one ended. Streaming video is a down and dirty way to convert to digital format. You probably would not want to share these DVDs, since it is better to spend some time editing them and giving family and friends a nice copy with effects, titles—the works.

you want—so that the final video, as you burn it to DVD, flows and tells the story of what happened at the family gathering or a child's band performance.

WHAT CAN I DIGITIZE FROM VIDEO?

Anything you have on videotape or camcorder tape can be converted to a digital image and then burned to DVDs or video CDs. The higher the quality of the original tape, the better the digitized version will be.

Family gatherings are something that everyone likes to see, and a visual copy of one might make a great present, especially if you have taken the time to not only digitize the original video but also to put in a title and some text so that, as the movie progresses, it isn't just a replay of the gathering. If you are particularly creative with the text, you may find that the family can't wait for you to digitize next year's gathering as well.

Remember that if you are going to go through all of this, in addition to preserving those videos, which is what you are doing to a certain extent, you should be having fun as you do it.

Reminder

SO HOW LONG DOES IT TAKE?

Digitizing video is not something that can be rushed. There is no high-speed dub option in video. Capturing a video takes as long as it would to play the video—so, if you wanted to capture twenty minutes of video then it would take you twenty minutes to do so. You may see this described in your video editor's manual as a 1:1 ratio. That is, it takes one minute to capture every one minute of video. However, once you get to the step of burning the digitized video to DVD or CD, be aware that this ratio is seldom as accurate as it is in capturing

BUNDLES

If you are planning on digitizing a lot of video, but do not have the necessary hardware and software yet, then you may find the bundle products save you money. Bundles are those products that combine some of the hardware with the necessary software. For instance, Pinnacle Studio <www.pinnaclesys.com> offers a number of bundles, the biggest difference being the connection cable that comes with the capture card and the software.

If you find a particular video-editing software that you want, see if it comes bundled with a capture card or DVD burner. Some of the bundles come with the burner instead of the capture cards. But anything that helps you save money while enabling you to do what you want is a smart buy.

Warning

the video on your computer. Your system is probably doing other things that are using some of its resources, so **generally you will find that the burn ratio is a little slower than the capture ratio, and it takes longer to burn the video.**

The time it takes to edit will depend on everything you want to do with the video you have captured. Are you just doing a "raw" capture? Or do you intend to work with the digitized copy to get rid of any dead spots or down times on the film, and to delete scenes where the camera is jumpy? Are you planning on adding fade-ins or fade-outs? Are you going to enhance the video so that you can see the people better? Do you want to add text?

The more editing you plan to do, the more time it will take you to do it. Just as scanning a photograph takes a couple of minutes from preview scan to save even if you do nothing additional to the image, and that time increases if you edit the photo to fix the scratches or enhance it in any way.

PLANNING FOR THE FUTURE

Once you have edited a few videotapes, you will find that you look at your videotapes differently. Concentrating on which scenes worked and which ones didn't becomes more apparent. You are not just sitting back watching a tape of the birthday party or family reunion. Instead, you are viewing moments of the videotape with a discerning eye.

The more time you spend working with these videos, the more ideas you will have about the types of shots you liked and what you want to do differently the next time you are videotaping the family. Some things to keep in mind:

- To avoid an unsteady hand, use a tripod whenever possible; unnecessary movement is distracting and could make your audience seasick.
- Natural light is best, but remember to try and keep the sun to your back if it is a sunny day.
- Keep panning and zooming to a minimum. When overused they actually

DVD MOVIE WRITER DC3000

If you are interested in streaming video, as opposed to editing before burning it to the DVD, then you may want to look at products like Hewlett-Packard's DVD Movie Writer dc3000 <www.hp.com>. This product allows you to record from any analog video source and write to a DVD. The DVD Movie Writer still needs to be connected to a computer, but it can also act as your general purpose CD and DVD writer. This unit does not sit in your computer, but on your desk. This may make popping the discs in and hooking up the camera a little easier than if you have installed an internal drive.

Figure 10-3
When the image is divided into thirds with a tic-tac-toe overlay, it is best to put the subject of your photo where two of the lines intersect.

draw the viewer's attention away from the subject or action on the video, and they can affect video compression during digitizing.

- Be sure to do some close-ups of your subjects. It gives the viewer the feeling that they are getting to know the person on the video or that they are included.

- Consider using a still-camera approach known as "the rule of thirds." The area that you can see is divided like a tic-tac-toe board, so you have nine squares. The subject should never be in the center, but off to one side or the other, and perhaps looking or interacting with something to the other side (see Figure 10-3 above).

- Consider "blocking" your shots before you begin videotaping. This means that you have an idea of some of the shots you want to get based on the event you are videotaping, and have tried to figure out the best places for you to be standing to get those shots.

SOME THINGS TO KEEP IN MIND WHEN CREATING DVDs

We have talked a lot about what is involved in creating DVDs. You have been introduced to necessary hardware and software and computer concerns. **Here are a few final thoughts about converting your videotapes to help you remember some important points and perhaps save a few steps.**

Notes

- VHS and analog camcorder tapes (8mm) must be converted to digital format. This is what the capturing part of the conversion process is all about. You might be able to save a little time with the smaller 8mm analog camcorder tapes if you now have a digital camcorder. Use the digital camcorder to convert the tapes. The digital camcorder will read the older tapes and convert them as it sends them to the computer, doing the first step for you.
- You must use USB 2 connection for any conversion box (like the HP Movie Writer we discussed earlier). The earlier, and slower, USB 1.1 is not fast enough to give you the high-quality video capture you want.
- Consider purchasing a separate hard drive just for the storing of the files as you are converting your videos. Remember—it takes a lot of space for even just a few minutes of video.
- Each DVD traditionally will hold about one hour of video. Keep this in mind when editing and compiling your finished masterpiece. The timeline built into the video editor will help you keep track of the total time of your project.
- If you want to record more than an hour on the DVD, some software packages will let you do this, but you will sacrifice quality in favor of the extra storage space.
- Remember that the capturing process is equal to the minutes being captured. The writing process to DVD can take longer.
- If you are creating DVDs for your family to play on the DVD players they have connected to their televisions, they may have trouble reading rewritable DVDs. Stick to those discs that are burned to only once.

CONVERTING YOUR AUDIOTAPES

Good news—converting your audiotapes doesn't take nearly as much in hardware, software, or computer resources as converting your videotapes does. So, you can breathe a sigh of relief where that is concerned. However, you will still be investing time in this project. So why do it?

Analog tapes, whether they are video or audio, will deteriorate. Eventually you will lose whatever is on those tapes. For genealogists this means losing a tangible piece of the past, and worse, perhaps the only recording you may have of your great-grandmother before she passed away. You don't want to lose that, so digitizing it and converting it to CD is the only option.

HARDWARE NEEDED

Just as you needed certain hardware to convert videotapes, there are certain things your computer needs to have to convert audiotapes, as well.

- Sound card—all computers have one of these, but your sound card will need to have a "line in" plug into which you can plug a cable from the audio cassette player. If you purchased your computer within the last five years it is likely that you already have the necessary plug. If your computer doesn't have the needed sound card, the good news is that they are relatively inexpensive and can be purchased at any computer store.
- Hard disk space—though digitizing audio is not nearly as intensive as the video, you still want to have lots of free hard disk space on your computer where the sound recorder software can store the converted audio file.
- CD burner—also referred to as a CD writer, this is similar to the DVD burner we already discussed. Once the audio has been converted from the cassettes, then the computer can burn it to a CD.

SOFTWARE

Before you buy software, see if you have anything that came with your computer. More and more, a variety of useful utilities are preinstalled on today's computers. It is possible that one of the utilities would be useful in converting audiocassettes and, therefore, you wouldn't need to purchase any other software.

Tip

If you have already invested in video-editing software to digitize your videotapes, you can use this same software in converting audiocassettes. However, if you aren't planning on converting any video, then you don't need to pay for the more expensive software. Just look for one of the programs exclusively intended for converting audiotapes.

IT'S DIGITIZED—NOW WHAT DO I DO?

The sound-recording software creates MP3 or WAV files that your computer will then be able to play using programs like Windows Media Player or Musicmatch Jukebox. Also, once the files are created on your computer, you can copy them onto a portable music device that plays these types of files.

When you digitize the voices of your relatives, a more creative idea is to incorporate the recording into a slideshow. Consider how mesmerized the family will be to listen to your great-grandmother reminiscing about her childhood as your slide show is displaying images of the old family homestead and the people she is talking about.

> **AUDIOTAPE CONVERTERS**
>
> These software packages can help you convert your audiotapes to .WAV files so that your computer can play them.
>
> - GoldWave <www.goldwave.com>
>
> - CD Wave <www.homepages.hetnet.nl/~mjmlooijmans/cdwave>
>
> - Total Recorder <www.highcriteria.com>
>
> - Sound Recorder Software <www.sound-recorder.com>

COMBINING IT ALL

Once you have converted your audio- and videotapes and scanned your photographs, then you actually can use a little from each to create personalized projects that share with other family members a glimpse of an ancestor or a family gathering. If your camcorder didn't capture an important moment in a wedding, for instance, but you had a still photo of the moment that you have now scanned, then you can incorporate that still photo into the final DVD project so it looks like it was meant to be that way.

Think about the many historical documentaries that use photographs of diaries and old pictures with voice-over narration. You have this same ability. You are limited only by your own imagination once the images are on the computer.

BEING CREATIVE

Up to this point, most of what we have talked about has been devoted to working on your desktop computer with a scanner and other peripherals that require power as well as connections to your computer. Let's look at some of the ways you can share your genealogy using printers and some unique programs.

ELEVEN

Printing and Sharing Your Digitized Images

T his, to me, is one of the best things about family history: sharing what you have found. In the past, we were all excited to be sharing charts of our family history. Today we can enhance that information so much more by adding pictures of our ancestors to some of those charts and creating wonderful slideshows that can be played at family reunions. No longer is genealogy a dry subject—instead, it is vibrant and full of color. There is movement and sound now and, with the right creativity, you can have your own family masterpiece on your hands.

When the picture pedigree first entered the scene in genealogy software, it was a novelty. Because few people had scanners then, it didn't take off like it would eventually. Now all genealogy programs offer some type of picture pedigree or photo tree, along with a whole host of other features. Colors abound in many of the charts and trees you can print out now, and there is no limit to how you can share your genealogy.

You may already have a printer that is capable of creating the best of reports and charts, but let's take a few moments to look at the different types of printers available, what each is best for, and how to select a printer based on the projects you have in the works.

A TISKET, A TASKET, A PRINTER IN MY BASKET

Shopping for printers is easier than it used to be because they have dropped considerably in price. But making a decision can still be difficult because there are so many different ones—each exclaiming perfection in one arena or another. Photographers look for high-end specialty photo printers. Newsletter publishers may look for a laser printer that offers a clean, crisp copy of which they can make multiple photocopies.

There are printers that appeal to all kinds of people—from the professional to the hobbyist and everyone in between, regardless of what their focus may be. Some printers use laser toner, similar to that of a photocopy machine, while others use a liquid ink that is sprayed onto the page. Deciding which is better depends largely on the project rather than a personal preference. And since the printers have come down in price it is often possible to have more than one type so that any project is possible. Of course, if you are going to spend your hard-earned money on printers to produce the family history you have labored to compile, you want it to look its very best.

LASER PRINTERS: NOT JUST FOR TEXT ANYMORE

In the past, the choice between inkjet and laser models was predetermined by whether or not you wanted to print in color. If you wanted to print a color picture then your only option was the inkjet. Then we began to hear rumors about color laser printers, and I say rumors because the price tag associated with them was so high that they were still a figment of imagination for most of us. That has changed, though, and quality color laser printers are now an affordable option, with many now available for the same price as a high-quality black laser printer.

It used to be that the laser printer offered a clearer print and was the preferred method for printing a family history when you were having it published, especially through one of the "vanity" type presses. Such presses required a camera-ready copy, and the laser printer, with its toner that stuck to a heated page, was the only printer at the time that offered such a high-quality print. In the late 1980s and early 1990s, color printers were reserved for specialty print shops, and it cost a lot to get anything printed in color. Actually, at that time, most genealogists who had personal computers were probably still using a dot matrix printer.

A laser printer then cost close to two thousand dollars and was something that only those with home offices that were set up for business, not a genealogy hobby, could afford. The dot matrix models did not produce nearly as clear a print, and the small dots making up the letters sometimes appeared quite obvious. But they were affordable. As the laser printer became less expensive, the dot matrix began to disappear from homes. Throughout the years the dot matrix printers have faded away.

The laser printer is still a quick, quality alternative (see Figure 11-1 on page 127). Most of the current laser printers can print upwards of ten to twelve pages a minute, and some of the additional features, such as duplex printing, help to keep the ever-growing pile of paper from consuming every corner of your office.

And while the toner cartridges usually cost around seventy dollars, most of them print upwards of three thousand to thirty-five hundred pages before

Definitions

DOT MATRIX PRINTERS

A *dot matrix printer* relies on pins or wires to strike a ribbon, much like a typewriter uses the force of the key striking the ribbon to transfer ink to the page. The number of pins of the dot matrix printer defines the quality of the printing. The more pins, the smaller they are, and the higher the quality is.

Definitions

DUPLEX PRINTING

If a laser printer has a *duplex printing* capability, it means the printer is designed to print on both sides of the page. This helps cut down on the number of pieces of paper you print, though it does not cut down on the amount of toner. It also may make printing slower as the printer sends each page through to print one side, then pulls it back, turns it over, and prints the other side.

needing to be replaced. This makes the laser printer a reasonably inexpensive printer in the long run.

I have seen some color laser printers recently for less than a thousand dollars. These models sometimes use up to four toner cartridges, one each of black, cyan, magenta, and yellow. Like the black laser printers, the number of pages each cartridge is supposed to be able to print is close to four thousand pages. And because the cartridges are separate, you need only replace the one that is out. Color laser printers also offer speedy black-and-white printouts, though these models are much slower when it comes to printing in color.

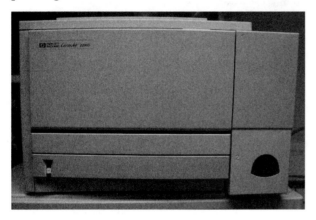

Figure 11-1
Laser printers are high capacity machines—some even offer paper drawers that hold five hundred sheets at a time.

ENTER THE INKJET

Some years back, as we were moving from dot matrix printers to laser printers, a new player came on the shelf—the inkjet. Early inkjet printers were, like their laser counterparts, black ink only. Instead of requiring high temperatures to adhere the toner to the paper, the inkjet, as its name implies, sprays the ink onto the page through extremely small jets.

Inkjet printers earned popularity because they were an inexpensive alternative for those who still couldn't afford the laser printer, but who wanted higher quality than a dot matrix printer offered. While they produced clearer results than the dot matrix, the ink didn't always spray as clearly or uniformly as possible. But for those who couldn't afford a laser printer, the inkjet was a nice compromise (see Figure 11-2 on page 128).

Soon, though, inkjet printers began offering something that the laser printers couldn't—color. The inkjets printed in color, and they still did it at a reasonable price. Everyone—genealogists included—flocked to purchase them. Consumers were so impressed with the idea of printing in color that they forgot to consider one of the big drawbacks to inkjet printers.

The inkjet, because it sprays liquid ink, has one major drawback for any printing—the ink is not waterproof. While this may not seem like a major issue, consider

Warning

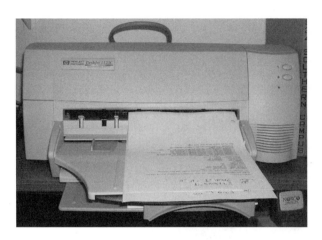

Figure 11-2
Inkjet printers bring vibrant colors to your output, while also printing black text.

what would happen if you have printed an envelope using an inkjet printer and then placed it outside for the mailman to pick up. In some places, outgoing mail is not protected by an enclosed mailbox, but left standing on end. If it rains, then there is potential for the ink to run and the address to be illegible.

By the same token, if you have printed some important information from a Web page devoted to one of the families you are researching, and a glass of water or other liquid is knocked over and the pages get wet, you have lost those pages.

This doesn't mean that we should stop using our inkjet printers, but you do need to consider their permanence—or lack thereof—when deciding what type of a printer you want to use for your project.

Money Saver

ARE YOU REALLY SAVING?

Keep in mind that inkjet printers are not designed for heavy printing. They often have a lower monthly "duty cycle"—that is, the maximum number of pages they can print in a month. While the printers cost less and the ink cartridges appear to cost half as much as toner cartridges, in the end the average cost per page is often the same as or more than that of a laser printer.

LET ME GIVE YOU PHOTOS

The most recent advance in printers is the photo-specific printer. Designed to offer digital camera fanciers an outlet for printing photo-quality pictures, they use inkjet technology in a DPI high enough to achieve that quality. Many photo printers actually double as traditional inkjet printers, handling many different types of paper—from those intended for inkjet printers to the glossy photo papers that help to improve the quality of the photo being printed.

There are a few different types of photo printers, and some are designed only to render standard photo sizes, including 3″×5″ and 4″×6″ photos. These small printers produce high-quality pictures and are portable (see Figure 11-3 on page 129). As long as you have access to a wall socket you may not even need a computer—many of them contain card readers, allowing you to go from camera to printer without a computer.

Photo printers were the first entry into the high-resolution output race. In order to match traditional photo quality, it was necessary that the cameras taking the pictures have a high resolution—thus the megapixels we now see attached to most cameras. Of course, if the printer couldn't handle the high resolution, it didn't matter how clear the image was that was taken by the camera, because you were limited to the resolution of the printer. Photo printers offer resolutions so high that, if you had a high-quality image to begin with, you may be able to enlarge the photo to an 8″ × 10″ size without noticing any image degradation.

Money Saver

PAPER MAKES THE DIFFERENCE

To ensure a high-quality photo is printed, make sure you are using good quality photo paper. I tend to use the paper sold by the company that made my printer, because in general most high quality paper costs about the same.

Figure 11-3
Photo printers come in many sizes and offer ways of printing without having a computer connected to the printer.

TONER AND INK REFILLS—DO YOU DARE?

The price tags of many of the toner and ink cartridges do come with a slight sticker shock, especially when you think about the fact that you have just paid thirty-five dollars for a small (1½″) square black box that almost disappears in a closed fist. Of course, the cost of the ink or toner cartridge needs to be considered over the long term. It is not thirty-five dollars for a single page, but for fifteen hundred pages, which averages out to about two cents per page. The seventy-dollar toner cartridge usually prints at least three thousand pages, again actually costing you around two cents per page. When you do the math, the price becomes a little more palatable.

This doesn't stop us from wanting to save some money when it comes to buying our ink or toner. Look in any computer magazine or visit any computer reseller, and you will see ads proclaiming the wave of the future, the only way you will save money when it comes to printers: refills. That's right, you buy just the toner or just the ink and refill your existing cartridge. Do they work? Some people swear by them, while others shy away. The companies that make the printers caution that, in order to get the high-quality output that you are seeking, you should only use their brand of ink or toner cartridge.

Money Saver

NO COMPUTER NEEDED

Photo printers that include card reader slots for standard media cards also have the ability to print without using a computer. Some photo printers offer small LCD panels so you can view the individual photos on the cards before you print them. Others allow you to print a low-resolution index sheet of all the images on the card—a 4″ × 6″ card can handle about twenty-eight thumbnail images—so that you can select just the images you want to print. You never have to go through your computer.

This is only an option if the images you are printing require no editing through your image-editing software. It is ideal for those times when perhaps you want to leave a set of prints with the family member you have been visiting who took you to the cemetery. (Hopefully, as you were taking the pictures with your digital camera you were looking at them to ensure you had some good shots before leaving the location.)

I like to set my small photo printer to a task completely disconnected from my computer and then work on a computer project while it is printing the photos for me. This way I am not tied up while the photo printer works, and neither do I see any slow down in the desktop or notebook computer from the printer using computer resources.

Tip

DO YOU REALLY NEED THE BEST QUALITY?

There are times when we do indeed want the very best quality our printer can give us. These times, though, are fewer than we think. Most of what we are printing is for our personal files and personal use. Such pages need not be printed at high quality. Most printers, both laser and inkjet, offer draft-quality printing options. In addition to saving a little on the toner or ink, you also will find that it increases the printing speed.

They will not guarantee the output if you use another company's cartridge or you refill an existing cartridge.

Refilling cartridges isn't always as easy as it may sound. In many instances it requires drilling a hole in the plastic housing of the cartridge that actually holds the ink or toner. Then there is the issue, especially with the ink cartridges, of the electronic components used in spraying the ink. The jets can get clogged, affecting the quality of your printed page. And the toner in the laser cartridges is particularly hazardous, not to mention extremely messy, if inhaled or spilled while filling the toner cartridge. Another negative to refilling inkjet ink is that it has the potential for fading much faster with these refill inks than with the ink developed by the people who developed the printer. When all is said and done you may find that the time and hassle of refilling is simply not worth what small savings such refills offer. And no amount of money would replace a photo that faded if you didn't have a way to print it again.

The vast array of printers available at a relatively economical price expands our printing opportunities. Creativity is boundless, limited only by your ability to create. Some printers come with tips, or you may find hints or suggestions on uses for your printer on the manufacturer's Web site. For genealogists, when printers are combined with the other gadgets, including scanners and digital cameras, then an ancestor is brought to life—or at least becomes a more three-dimensional person. All of this technology is a way for us to share glimpses into the lives and gatherings of our families.

SCRAPBOOKING AND STILL PRESERVING

Scrapbooking is a popular pastime. There are magazines devoted to this hobby. Many genealogists either got into genealogy because of their enthusiasm for scrapbooking or got into scrapbooking because of their enthusiasm for family history—and a longing to share more than just names, dates, and places. Regardless of which way it went, scrapbooking is intended to take the many family pictures and create a book that is representative of a person, family, reunion, or special event. Scrapbooks allow such people and events to be remembered long after they have begun to fade in the memories of those who were present, and offer a glimpse of what they were like to those who were not present.

In the past, scrapbooking required using original records and photographs in the creation of those memory books. Elaborate scissors are available to assist scrapbookers in designing unique, eye-catching frames for the pictures, which were then glued into the scrapbook. I can already see a few of you grimacing at the idea of original photographs, perhaps old photographs, being treated in this manner.

By scanning and printing the original photos, you can scrapbook to your heart's content while still preserving the original photographs. In fact, scanning the photos and working with digitized duplicates offers many opportunities to use the same photograph or portions of it throughout the project. You even could create identical scrapbooks for each member of the family, or you might want to cut the duplicate photos instead of relying solely on paper frames to give the scrapbook that personal touch.

Some scrapbookers like that hands-on approach to creating their scrapbook.

Important

GO ONLINE

While the Internet seems to have something for everyone, if you find that no one has created a site dedicated to what you are interested in, create your own—others who share your interest will quickly find you. That's sort of what happened to Denis Germain. He posted a message on the message boards at Two Peas in a Bucket <www.twopeasinabucket.com> and from there ended up with his own site, <www.escrappers.com>.

E-SCRAPBOOK PROGRAMS

Scrapbook Factory Deluxe <www.novadevelopment.com> is a Windows program that brings everything a scrapbooker could want to e-scrapbooking. It offers more than 2,500 exclusive templates and customizable projects, more than twenty thousand graphics, five hundred fonts, a built-in digital photo editor, embellishments, text effects, and other features, and all for less than fifty dollars.

Ulead's My Scrapbook <www.ulead.com> is another Windows program with power. It offers customizable scrapbook-theme pages, more than three hundred clip art items, the ability to create background paper, fonts, and a built-in photo editing program—all for about twenty-five dollars.

Important

PROTECTING PRIVACY

While legally you do not have to protect the privacy of your living relatives, ethically it is something you should consider. If we are mindful to keep information we have about our living family members out of the public eye, those same family members might be more willing to share information about the family with you. Don't give them an excuse to blame you for "identity theft," or for the potential for such, by sharing their information on the Internet.

However, there are some great ways to create a scrapbook completely on your computer. You may find you have even more fun, because the scrapbooking software may give you some great ideas for the ultimate finished product.

Earlier we talked about how you can scan anything, including your heritage items. With e-scrapbooking, you can use those family heirloom materials as backgrounds or as frames around the digital images. And don't forget the clip art that is available on CD at extremely low costs. You'll soon find that almost anything on your computer can be incorporated into your e-scrapbook.

Scrapbooking is just one of the ways you can share the photos, records, and other memorabilia you have accumulated in your research. Once you have digitized your family's history, there are no limits to what you can do.

A family reunion invitation takes on a personalized note when you enhance it with pictures of ancestors. Newsletters can now do more than just tell you what happened at the reunion; they can show you. Your published family history not only states the family connections, but offers proof through the digitized records that can now be included without fear of them being illegible. Sharing was never so easy, and never had so many possibilities.

IF IT'S DIGITIZED, THE COMPUTER CAN USE IT

We limit ourselves because we think in traditional methods. So, when you think about sharing your family history, the first thing that comes to mind is a printed volume. And let me not discourage this as one form in which you can share your family history. Despite the advances in technology it is still the most reliable method, and it certainly has the longest shelf life. At least once during your genealogy hobby, be sure to create some book or booklet of the family tree and then donate copies of it to the Family History Library—

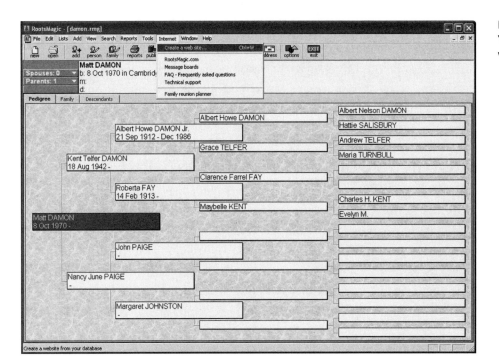

Figure 11-4
You can create a Web site
with the click of a button.

with permission to microfilm—and any other public or specialty libraries you feel would appreciate having a copy.

Of course, while you continue to research and compile that tree, there are other ways to share or publish the information that are not quite so permanent. They also allow you to edit as your research progresses and to reach many individuals, some of whom may be able to offer additional records or information (see Figure 11-4 above).

Idea Generator

While all genealogy programs offer some Web page creation ability, they may not offer the means to include all the images that you would like to use in the creation of those pages. Some of the programs may offer you options to include more images before they create the Web pages, but if not, that's okay. After creating the Web pages using your genealogy program—which does the hard part—open them in a Web editing program (there are many to choose from) to add in the other images of records and people that you want to include.

Once you have digitized photographs, scanned documents, or taken digital pictures of tombstones, then your computer can use them in any way, and the Web is a perfect place for genealogists to share some of these images. But in order to publish them to the Web, you will need to change the resolution of the images. Unlike printed versions, the Web copies do not need the high detail, nor can most people's computers handle the download of the extremely large files that contain the high-resolution images.

In most instances, when uploading graphics to the Internet, all you need is a 72-dpi image because it keeps the size of the file down and is still detailed enough for your monitor. Changing the resolution can be done in any graphics program, so whatever program you are using to edit, crop, or restore your pictures can be used to change the resolution. Then you will have the high-resolution image for printing photos and also a low-resolution image for sharing online.

CREATING YOUR OWN FAMILY HISTORY CD

Another way you may want to share your genealogy is by burning it onto a CD. Most computers in the last few years have come with a writable compact disc unit that makes it possible for you to create your masterpiece on the computer in a number of different ways, and then burn it to CD. This is an inexpensive way to share your genealogy with your extended family.

Some of the creative options available include:

- Creating a narrative in your genealogy program and then exporting it to a PDF file.
- Working in a word processing program to create a book, and then saving that book in an HTML format to make navigation easy.
- Using a scrapbook or other specialty program to create a unique family history CD.

\di'fin\ vb

Definitions

PDF

PDF stands for *portable document format* and is a method of retaining the look and feel of a document as though it were sent to the printer. Because the Acrobat Reader is a free program that handles PDF documents, most people can open a PDF file when you are sharing your information in that format.

CREATING A PDF FILE

If you are planning on creating many different genealogy projects and you want complete flexibility in creating PDF files from almost any software application on your computer, then you will want to investigate purchasing Adobe Acrobat <www.adobe.com>. While the Adobe Acrobat Reader is a free download, the program that actually creates the PDF files is something that must be purchased, though it is not inexpensive.

Another way to create PDF files is a built-in PDF ability now found in

A CHEAPER ALTERNATIVE

If you can't justify the price tag of Adobe Acrobat, and really just want a simple way to create PDF files without being able to edit them after they are created, then you may want to look at these alternatives:

- pdfFactory <www.fineprint.com>
- CutePDF <www.acrosoftware.com/Products/CutePDF/Printer.asp>
- Pdf995 <www.pdf995.com>

many genealogy programs. **One thing to understand about such PDF files is that if you do not have the Acrobat program to edit the file, then once the file is created by the genealogy program, there is no way to alter it.** This means you should take your time creating the report in your genealogy program before you convert it to PDF form. Of course, the plus to creating these on the computer instead of printing them out is that, if you aren't happy with the PDF file, you simply delete it and create a new one.

WORKING IN YOUR WORD PROCESSOR

Another way to share your family history, especially if your genealogy program won't let you upload your Web page anywhere that you want, is to create the narrative report in your genealogy program and then export it in an RTF format. With an RTF-formatted report, you can open it in your word processing program and add additional images or family stories. The hard part—the formatting of the genealogy report and the handling of the source footnotes—already has been done for you.

Most word processors now offer a save-to-HTML format that takes the document and creates the appropriate HTML-coded file for uploading to the Internet, or for burning to a CD, so that it is viewable in any Web browser software.

The benefit in working in your word processing program is that you are probably familiar with the program and understand how to add graphics and format text. You actually may feel more comfortable working in the word processor than you would have in your genealogy program. The word processor also may have more functionality than any text editor that is built into the genealogy program.

SCRAPBOOKS OR SPECIALTY PROGRAMS

I am always amazed at the many different programs that are created each year. While the big office suites and games seem to get the most advertising time, there are some great programs that are in hiding. A few of the graphics programs previously mentioned come immediately to my mind, as do the great genealogy programs that we have discovered in our quest for our family tree.

There are so many other programs, though, including e-journals, e-scrapbooks, and other ways to share your family history through digitized pictures, histories, and audio and video. You can always turn to some of the traditional graphic editing programs, such as those that we have already mentioned, or you might want to look at a program like Family History CD <www.family historycd.com>. This inexpensive program offers quite a bit of power to your

Warning

\di'fin\ *vb*

Definitions

RTF

RTF stands for *rich text format*, and is a document file format that retains a great deal of formatting but can be opened in any word processing program that supports this type of file. Most word processing programs can both open and save this type of file.

\di'fin\ *vb*

Definitions

HTML

HTML stands for *Hyper Text Markup Language.* It is the code behind the Web pages you view in your Web browser software. The software converts the code into the text, graphics, fonts, colors, and placement you see on the screen.

fingertips when it comes to creating a treasure of family history information (see Figure 11-5 below). Through a series of menu items, this program allows you to build elaborate collections of digitized photos, to include video and histories (in almost any format, though regular text files or PDF files are probably the best), and to burn it all to a CD.

Figure 11-5
Family History CD gives you the tools you need to put together an interactive CD of your family history to share with relatives.

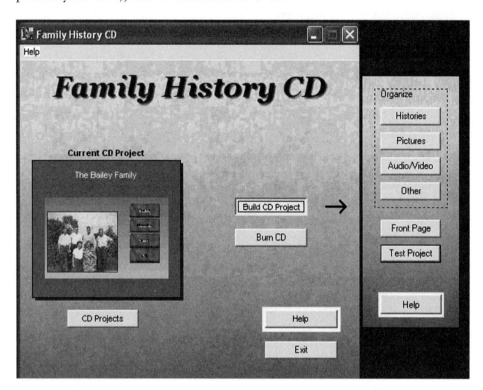

Idea Generator

Using the Family History CD program allows you to create a viewable CD for anyone you wish to share the family history with. You can also add a GEDCOM file, which can then be opened by the person's own genealogy program. I prefer to create many different trees, charts, and reports in my genealogy program and export them in PDF file to a CD. This way the individual I share with need not have a genealogy program to enjoy the information I am passing along. After all, my mother and brother are not actively seeking their family history, but they are interested in what I find and in the pictures I have accumulated. Sharing that with them through a Family History CD means that all they have to do is pop the CD in and run it. Family History CD includes all the files necessary for anyone to view the creation—you do not have to own the program.

While I continue to share my information on the Internet and through some of the many other avenues already discussed, I will confess that at some point I hope to publish a book of the family history using a quality genealogy publisher, such as Gateway Press, which is affiliated with Genealogical Publishing Company <www.genealogical.com>.

PUBLISHING THE FAMILY HISTORY

I think we all hope to publish our family histories in some more permanent method beyond the Internet. While the Internet is a great way to reach out to cousins and gather additional information during the research and compilation phases, at some point we should publish a printed version of our family history to donate to a few libraries. Using a professional press such as Gateway costs some money, but it gives you a hardbound record of all of your hard work and passion. There may be a good printer who lives in your town who might also be willing to create a book for you. You may also want to investigate the various options now available with those companies that offer print-on-demand.

Whenever you are printing your images and graphics, be sure to use the high-resolution graphics you created during the scanning or photo-taking aspect of your research. This guarantees that the images, provided they are printed with a good printer (preferably a laser printer), will look clear and will duplicate well.

If you want to donate your family history to libraries, creating a printed volume is the best approach. Technology changes rapidly, and libraries will not be able to upgrade your personal family history even if they accept it in CD format in the first place. The book, however, will continue to be useful to future researchers regardless of how computers and technology change ten, thirty, or even fifty years from now.

ON THE MOVE AGAIN

The road warrior, who is out there amassing many of the records and photos that will eventually be used in some of the projects discussed here, has many goodies with her as she goes around digitizing and gathering more information. We have touched on some of them already in earlier chapters and have shown how we can use some of those in sharing the family history. Now its time to look at the tiny modern marvels that let us take our genealogy with us, so that we have it on hand regardless of whether or not we had planned to have a genealogy moment.

Definitions

GEDCOM

GEDCOM stands for Genealogy Data Communication. This allows genealogy programs to share data without the genealogist having to type in the information. The genealogy program reads each line of the GED file—a standard text file—and puts the genealogical information in the appropriate fields.

For More Info

WRITING YOUR FAMILY HISTORY

To find out more about writing and publishing your family history, see Sharon De-Bartolo Carmack's *You Can Write Your Family History* (Cincinnati: Betterway Books, 2003).

TWELVE

Taking Your Genealogy With You

T he genealogical road warrior knows his limitations when it comes to traveling to get the next ancestor. There may be some walls to climb over or barriers to get around, but the genealogical road warrior always gets his man, or woman, in the end. We already talked about some of the tools that make traveling a little easier, and in chapter seven I described my road warrior kit. In that kit, I mentioned PDAs—personal digital assistants—but I didn't go into any detail about them. They are such a powerful tool in such a small package that I feel they deserve to be set apart.

For years, personal digital assistants, PDAs, were just that—small electronic devices intended to help you keep track of your daily appointments and tasks. Many people moved from paper schedules or organizers to the earliest of the PDAs. Over time, just as we have seen with all the other technology, the PDA has evolved and become much more than an electronic nag that you have to go the dentist again.

Reminder

Today's PDAs offer much more than a calendar, task list, and note section. There are developers who design programs just for these little mini-computers, and mini-computers they are. Don't be fooled by their size—today's PDAs are powerful little dynamos that offer many features and many applications to choose from.

Not only can I take my genealogy with me, I can now add to my genealogy, or at least make notes that I can then put into my laptop later. Of course this may bring up a question—why do you need a PDA at all if you have a laptop? You may not need a PDA. But I find that there are times when it can go into an archive or repository where my notebook can't. I also have my PDA with me all the time; it's with me in my purse when I am home and goes in the road warrior kit when I travel.

The notebook always goes with me when I travel, but I don't always find that I can use it when inspiration strikes. Having much of my information in the PDA offers me the opportunity to record my thoughts or double-check a fact when I am in a cemetery, or simply guides me to the next turn as I drive to an unfamiliar location. My PDA can do all of this and a whole lot more.

PALM VS. POCKET PC

PDAs come with one of two operating systems. Just as you find computers and laptops running either Windows or Macintosh operating systems, with PDAs you will find your choice is between Windows Mobile 2003 for Pocket PC, more commonly known as Pocket PC, and the Palm operating system. There are some considerable differences between the two.

The Palm operating system was actually the first of these pocket-sized operating systems. As such, it is possible that through your employer you were introduced to one a few years ago. Many companies purchased Palm devices for their employees in an effort to streamline certain aspects of the business. Palm devices traditionally offer their users a place to record appointments, to-do lists, and addresses. Many of the Palm products have hot spots for these specific applications.

A HISTORY OF THE PALM

For many years Palm seemed to have the market for handheld computers, or personal digital assistants, all to itself. And to a large degree this was correct. By 2001, Palm actually had 90 percent of the market share. Today, in addition to the Palm company, there are a few others, such as Sony, that use the Palm operating system. Palm traces its beginnings to 1992, when Jeff Hawkins founded the company. His goal was to create a device that would be of use to the general public in tracking appointments, logging phone numbers, etc. He achieved what he set out to do, especially when it came to synchronizing the PDA with a computer and in his handwriting recognition program. Known as Graffiti, this program relies on the person entering letters to use certain lines and directions, which the Palm recognizes as letters. Perhaps not as ambitious as some of the other handhelds, with its emphasis on an address book, planner, to-do list, and memo capability, it is still a popular product, and new features continue to be added. The growing availability of add-on programs offers even more functionality to the Palm.

The Pocket PC operating system more closely resembles the Windows operating system, and this is by design, since both are developed by Microsoft. Whereas the Palm was originally both the operating system and the device, Pocket PC has always been the operating system that developers of handheld devices licensed for use in their PDAs. Like the Palm, Pocket PC devices offer places to record

Reminder

A LOOK AT THE ORIGINS OF POCKET PC

Pocket PC is Microsoft's handheld operating system. It has gone through a few name changes since it was released as Windows CE in 1997. Despite the huge jump that Palm has had in this market, Microsoft hopes that in the next few years Pocket PC will become Palm's equal. The Pocket PC interface is like a light version of Windows. In fact, PDAs running the Pocket PC operating system also come with Pocket Word and Pocket Excel versions of these two popular pieces of the Microsoft Office suite. While the latest versions of Pocket PC have begun to recognize handwriting, it is not as thorough with its recognition as Palm, due in part to the fact that Pocket PC is trying to understand what you have written. Palm avoids this problem through Graffiti, which requires you to conform to a given method of writing the letters. The screens of most Pocket PCs are also bigger than the Palm counterparts, because they do not have to have a place for the user to write the Graffiti marks. The Pocket PC uses a small keyboard that the user taps on with the stylus, or, in some of the programs, free-hand writing can be used.

---

appointments, to-do lists, and addresses. They also come standard with "lite" versions of Word and Excel to make transferring of such documents from your computer to your PDA possible.

There are some major differences between the two operating systems, though I often think it is more the mindset of the individual that is the ultimate deciding factor as to which device the person settles on. As you can see in the picture of the two devices, one of the first noticeable differences is the size of the screen (see Figure 12-1 on page 141). At first glance it would appear that the screen on both is about the same size—however, the viewable area on the Palm device is much smaller. This is to allow for the Graffiti panel on the Palm. The Graffiti handwriting was one of the major advances with the Palm devices. Instead of trying to teach the device to recognize many different writing styles, the developer of the Palm operating system decided it would be easier to teach the user of the device a different writing style— enter Graffiti. In fact, when I opened the box in which my Sony Clié came, one of the first things I found was my Graffiti card that showed me how to write not only letters but numbers, punctuation marks, and a host of other characters.

The overall feel to the operating systems is quite different as well, as is the way in which it handles extended memory slots. The Pocket PC is a little easier when it comes to having extra memory slots for SD or CompactFlash cards. With the Pocket PC operating system, as I install new programs I can put them and their data on the memory card and run it from there. With the Palm device, I notice that while I have space for a memory card, which with the Sony is limited to the Sony Memory Stick, I must use an add-on program to move data back and forth. For most of the programs on the Palm, data can be stored on the memory stick, but it cannot be accessed or used from there. So while I can have a lot of data on the memory stick, I must move files back and forth to use them.

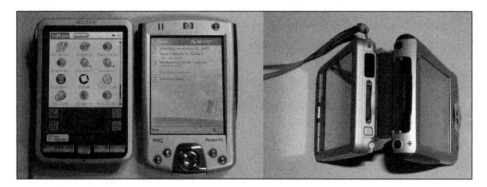

Figure 12-1
PDAs, such as this Sony Clié (Palm) and HP iPAQ (Pocket PC), give you power in your hand and sometimes offer memory card slots to increase the storage capacity.

IT'S ALL IN THE MIND

In asking some colleagues what prompted them to make the decision they did in selecting a Pocket PC device or a Palm device, it became clear that it was truly a mindset. I noticed that those individuals who used a traditional organizer often leaned first toward the Palm device. Their mindset was to simply get a more portable method of taking their daily planner with them, and the Palm's history shows that it was designed with this goal in mind.

WHO'S MAKING PDAS?

You will find information about the different Palm and Pocket PC varieties of PDAs by visiting the following developers' Web sites:

- Casio (Pocket PCs) <www.casio.com>

- Dell (Pocket PCs) <www.dell.com>

- Hewlett-Packard (Pocket PCs) <www.hp.com>

- Palm (Palm) <www.palm.com>

- Sony (Palm) <www.sonystyle.com>

- Toshiba (Pocket PC) <www.toshiba.com>

Those who tended to lean toward the Pocket PC devices saw them as an extension of their computer. They wanted to be prepared for times when they might have free time on their hands to continue working on a project, but could not use their notebook, and thus liked the idea of programs like Pocket Word. While not as robust as its desktop counterpart, in a pinch it fits the bill perfectly, at least for the initial draft of an article.

KEEPING CONNECTED

Important

Both Palm and Pocket PC devices come with some method of connecting them to your desktop or notebook computer. For some, this involves a cradle with a cable that connects to the computer. The cradle is also where you put the PDA when you are recharging its batteries. A few models are making it even easier by using just a cable that connects to both the PDA and the computer. The Sony Clié uses a special dongle into which both the USB cable and the power cable connect, no cradles. Still others ship with the cradle, but you then can purchase travel cables that allow you to recharge or connect to your notebook while you are on the road. The cradles add weight, so I prefer to spend the few extra dollars to get the additional cables. This also guarantees that I don't forget the all important power cables when I am on the road, because these cables stay packed all the time, ready to go with me, and the cradle stays on the desk in my office waiting for my return.

DONGLE

A *dongle* is a security device that attaches to a computer or PDA through the ports available on the device. In the past dongles were used as keys that launched certain applications. The program would not start until it had verified that the dongle was attached. While this is the traditional meaning of a dongle, on the consumer side of computers it is generally used to refer to any type of computer plug that plugs into the computer or other device and then allows a cable or something else to plug into it on the other side, facilitating the passing of information from the computer to the device and vice versa.

Most of the time, when you get a new program or want to backup the appointments, addresses, and tasks you have entered into the PDA, then you must connect it to your desktop or notebook computer. When you purchase a PDA it comes with software that allows this communication: ActiveSync for the Pocket PC, and HotSync for the Palm. It is also through these communication programs that you add new programs to your device and sometimes move files as well.

A PLETHORA OF PROGRAMS

Because the Palm has been around much longer, it is possible that you will find many more applications for it than for the Pocket PC. There are some twelve thousand software programs that can be run on Palm devices. However, I have noticed many programs that for years were exclusive to Palm are now offering Pocket PC editions as well. So, whereas in the past we might have picked a PDA based on the software we could run on it, now that is seldom a deciding factor.

If you are thinking about purchasing a PDA and have not purchased one in the past, then I encourage doing a little research. There are a number of Web sites that offer descriptions of the Palm and Pocket PC environments, and that give insight into the types of applications you can run on them. Understanding the limitations of both operating systems is useful when it comes time to select the one you want. Also, realizing that you may be unable to use certain programs on one or that some software works differently on each model may affect which type of device you select.

WHERE TO TURN FOR INFORMATION

There are many publications and online publications devoted to PDAs and other computer subjects, including:

- *Handheld Computing* <www.hhcmag.com>

- *Laptop* <www.techworthy.com>

- *PC World* <www.pcworld.com>

- *Pen Computing* <www.pencomputing.com>

- *Pocket PC Magazine* <www.pocketpcmag.com>

- *Smart Computing* <www.smartcomputing.com>

In general, though, the software abounds, and you will be hard-pressed to find that you can't find a particular application when you want it, even if it isn't made by the same developer as your notebook software. Some lesser-known companies offer equivalent programs at a fraction of the cost of the household name developers.

If you think you have settled on a particular model or brand, I don't encourage ordering it online, at least not until you have done one more thing: Visit your local computer and office supply stores to see what devices they offer for sale. Most of these devices will be plugged in, which allows you an opportunity to try them there. See if you can get to the address book or the calendar section. What other programs were you able to find already installed? Did you find the interface easy to use or frustrating? Your answer to this question is probably the best barometer as to how well you would enjoy the device in the end. If

Warning

PDA PROGRAMS FOR SALE ONLINE

There are many Web sites where you will find programs specifically devoted to PDAs. Most of them offer you trial versions of the products. It is a good idea to download the trial version before you pay for it so that you can make sure that it does what you expected and that it runs on your PDA system.

- Handango (Palm and Pocket PC programs) <www.handango.com>

- Handmark (Palm and Pocket PC programs) <www.handmark.com>

- PalmGear (Palm programs) <www.palmgear.com>

- PDA Street (Palm and Pocket PC programs) <www.pdastreet.com>

- PocketGear (Pocket PC programs) <www.pocketgear.com>

- Tucows (Palm and Pocket PC programs) <www.tucows.com>

a product frustrates you, then even if you figure out how to use it, you will probably never truly enjoy it.

Once you have done this, if you find a good deal on the Internet for the particular brand that you are interested in, then by all means, save the money by ordering online. Don't forget to factor in the shipping, though. Sometimes ordering online is no cheaper than going to the store and purchasing it on the spot—and online ordering comes with a longer wait.

ANCESTORS ANYTIME

For genealogists, the carrot where the PDA is concerned may be the fact that you can take your family history with you—anywhere. A number of programs available for both the Palm and the Pocket PC at the least let you take what you already know with you, and at the most allow you to add new data. Some developers are beginning to offer other programs useful to genealogists, including those designed for recording tombstone inscriptions or making journal entries (see Figure 12-2 on page 145).

If you already have a PDA and didn't know such programs existed, then you will find the list of programs on page 145, based on operating systems, a good place to start. Many of them offer trial versions, which means you can download the programs without buying them. This gives you the opportunity to verify that the program will run on your specific PDA configuration and that you feel comfortable with the interface. Although they are genealogy programs, the fact that they are being used on some simple devices often

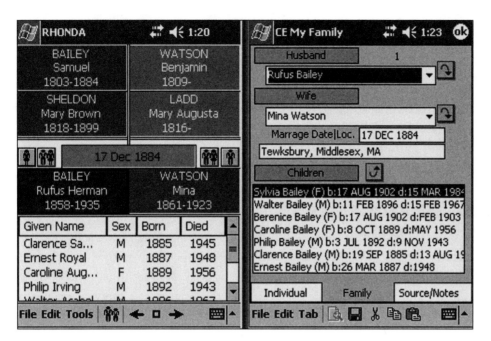

Figure 12-2
Pocket PC genealogy programs such as Pocket Genealogist (left) and CE My Family (right) allow you to take your family history with you.

alters what you can do with them and how you view the information (see Figure 12-3 below).

One of the nice things about most of the PDA software is the price. When it comes to genealogy software, you will find that the prices are quite reasonable for the programs listed below.

- CE My Family (Pocket PC) <www.cemyfamily.com>
- GedStar (Palm OS) <www.ghcssoftware.com/gedstar.htm>
- GedWise (Palm OS) <www.batteryparksoftware.com>
- My Roots (Palm OS) <www.tapperware.com/MyRoots>
- Personal Ancestral File Data Viewer (Palm OS) <www.familysearch.org>
- Pocket Genealogist (Pocket PC) <www.northernhillssoftware.com/pgenie.htm>

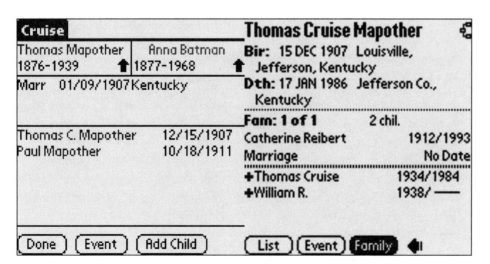

Figure 12-3
Palm genealogy programs are also available, including MyRoots (left) and GedWise (right).

Most genealogy PDA programs work from a GEDCOM file created on your notebook or desktop computer. Some of them then run that file through a program that resides on the desktop computer, which creates the PDA file. Some of the programs expect the PDA to be connected to the computer, while others create a holding file of sorts that will be placed on the PDA the next time you run the synchronization program between the computer and the PDA.

OTHER PROGRAMS

Although I find myself pulling out the PDA and opening my genealogy database frequently, when it comes to my PDA I spend more time using some additional programs to aid me with my research. A favorite pastime of mine is to walk through cemeteries, transcribing tombstones or simply marveling at those who have gone before, wondering what their lives were like. Admitting this in mixed company—genealogists and nongenealogists—usually garners nods from the fellow family historians and looks of concern from the nongenealogists. I am sure they have come to the conclusion that a short stay in a nice quiet room with soft walls would certainly be a good thing for me. A recent cruise club trip with the family to the Bahamas made that abundantly clear.

I was quite excited about being in the Bahamas. While I hadn't looked forward to the crossing, and with good reason—I have a healthy respect for Mother Nature—once we were there I began to plan some side trips to many of the smaller islands near the marina where we were staying. Each island

---

I DON'T WANT A GENEALOGY PROGRAM ON MY PDA

If you want to carry some of your genealogical information on your PDA but you are not interested in installing an actual genealogy program, you may want to consider using a spreadsheet. Some genealogy programs, such as Family Tree Maker, allow you to export the information from the genealogy program in a spreadsheet style that programs such as Microsoft's Excel can open.

If you create such a list, you can either tell your Palm software that you want to copy it to the Palm device, or you can put the file in the Pocket PC documents folder on your computer, from where it gets copied to the PDA the next time you use the auto-sync program. To open the file, your PDA needs to support the spreadsheet file format. With Pocket PC this is not a problem, as your PDA should have come with Pocket Excel preinstalled. With a Palm, you need to look into getting a third-party program such as Documents To Go <www.dataviz .com> to view the spreadsheet.

had its own cemetery, and I couldn't wait to visit them. Some of them had tombstones dating back to the 1700s. Upon my return from the first trip to a cemetery, one of the other members of the cruise club asked me if I had "gotten my fill of cemeteries." I smiled and shook my head. I had gone with my digital camera and had taken a host of photos of tombstones of people I am not related to, but by whom I am now fascinated, especially after seeing the destruction of the island from one of the hurricanes.

Throughout the rest of the trip, I made a few more side stops at small islands. Fortunately for me, the islands that we went to were so small that I could easily travel on foot and find the cemeteries. I did have a little help from satellites in the sky, but more about that later. By the end of the trip I'd been to three different islands and seen four cemeteries. I'd also picked up a published genealogy on some of the early Bahamian families, and I now look forward to spending a little time connecting the tombstones I have pictures of to the families in the book.

During that trip, I concentrated on the camera. Being in the boat for such a long time, packing was minimal, so I had left many of my gadgets at home. The camera and notebook computer—on which I kept my running journal of some of the events and places we had been to, including my sojourns in the cemeteries—were all I could bring.

I did miss the chance I usually have of transcribing the harder-to-read tombstones in my PDA. **On my Palm resides a nifty little program called Cemetery, created by Donald Keiffer and found on John One One Graphics' Web site at <www.keifferusa.com>, for transcribing tombstones.** I love to have it handy when I am in the cemetery and am concerned a picture may not be as readable as I'd like—even after viewing it on the display of the digital camera (see Figure 12-4 below).

Internet Source

Figure 12-4
Cemetery programs such as Donald Keiffer's Cemetery for the Palm let you transcribe tombstones in the palm of your hand.

THERE'S A GEEK IN THE CEMETERY

I am sure I paint an interesting picture to any passersby whenever I spend time in the cemetery. Armed with my Pocket PC, Palm PDA, and digital camera, I work my way from stone to stone or begin the search for a specific person. I can't help wondering if perhaps there is a neon sign that flashes over me to warn anyone nearby that there is a geek in the cemetery.

I have the digital camera for taking the pictures of the tombstones. I have the Palm PDA for transcribing the tombstones when they are difficult to read and I want to make sure I have an accurate transcription. I also use Donald Keiffer's Cemetery program to record the *global positioning satellite* (GPS) coordinates for that tombstone. And how do I get those coordinates? That's where the Pocket PC PDA comes in.

MY GPS KNOWS EXACTLY WHERE I AM

My GPS system allows me to know exactly where I am at any moment, provided I have a GPS receiver and a map upon which the GPS coordinates are displayed. GPS systems are not new. In fact, the military has been using them for years. GPS systems that can be purchased by civilians use the same satellites as the military systems do. GPS systems for the general public have been around for a while, too, though until recently most of them required a notebook computer.

While you still need a desktop or notebook computer to install the main program from which you will get the maps you need to load onto the PDA,

---

STAND ALONE GPS SYSTEMS

If the idea of using a global positioning satellite system appeals to you but you would rather not use a PDA, you have other options. Many GPS products on the market are stand-alone systems designed to lead you on your way. You simply tell the system your point of origin and your destination. GPS products are available for travel by land, air, and sea, and each one requires different types of reference points.

- DeLorme <www.delorme.com>

- Garmin <www.garmin.com>

- Lowrance Electronics <www.lowrance.com>

- Magellan <www.magellangps.com>

- Navman <www.navman.com>

once the maps are there, you are on your way. **These GPS systems can guide you from a hotel to a cemetery, giving you turn-by-turn directions—and pointing out your mistake if you didn't pay attention when it told you to make that right turn back there.** And depending on how detailed the maps are that come with the particular system you purchase, you may even be able to mark individual tombstones within the cemetery on the map you downloaded onto the PDA (see Figure 12-5 below).

My husband and I have been traveling by GPS for years. We have a couple of GPS receivers that we can attach to our notebook computers, and through DeLorme's Street Atlas program <www.delorme.com/streetatlasusa> we have been guided on many a trip. Not surprisingly, we also rely on a special GPS device on our boat when heading out in open water, and it works much better on the water than it does on land, as I discovered when trying to use it in the Bahamas to find a cemetery on an extremely small island (and no, I don't want to admit how long it took me to find the cemetery as I tried to follow the arrow on that GPS).

Recently I decided to invest in a GPS receiver for my PDA. I liked the idea of having something small that could travel with me and be available anywhere. When I initially purchased the WorldNavigator GPS by TeleType <www.teletype.com>, I had a different Pocket PC PDA. The WorldNavigator

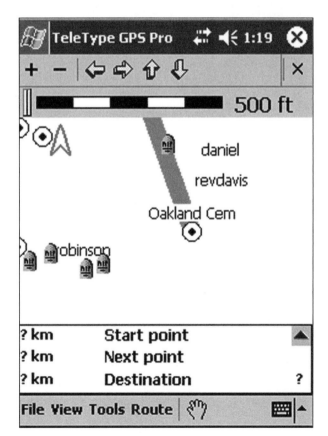

Figure 12-5
A good GPS program, such as Teletype's WorldNavigator, will let you pinpoint individual tombstones on the maps for later reference.

uses the CompactFlash slot for the GPS receiver. A problem I quickly discovered was that I was often too limited in the number of maps I could download to my PDA—limited by the onboard memory, since I had to remove my CompactFlash card because it uses the same slot as the GPS receiver.

Fortunately I was also in the market for a new Pocket PC PDA, which is my PDA of choice, and the GPS receiver played a major part in the one I ultimately settled on. I realized I would need one that had more than just a CompactFlash slot. The one I settled on, an iPAQ by HP, has a slot for CompactFlash and another slot for an SD card. So now I can load the maps on the SD card, giving me access to a lot more memory, while the GPS receiver sits in the CompactFlash slot.

In deciding on the GPS receiver and software that I would purchase I had similar criteria, as my husband found out. Since my birthday was coming soon, I put the WorldNavigator on my birthday list—you are never too old to have a birthday list—and it makes shopping easier for my husband. I also pointed out to him that he would have to order it off the Internet because it was not available at any of our local computer stores. He asked me about another one— one he could buy locally—and I calmly explained that the particular brand he asked about didn't do what I wanted. Before settling on the WorldNavigator, I had done my homework. I wanted a GPS receiver and maps that not only would get me to the cemetery, but also would let me pinpoint individual tombstones within the cemetery. This required that the software allow me to zoom in considerably. When I contacted TeleType, they responded almost immediately to my question and gave me additional information about their maps and where I could get more information about how detailed they were.

Reading reviews of other GPS packages for the Pocket PC, I discovered that the reviewer thought that one other packet was a little faster, and another had a couple of added bonuses that the package I wanted didn't. However, after using it, I find I am quite happy with it. It does what I wanted:

- Offers me door-to-door directions.
- Includes many points of interest, including cemeteries, libraries, historical buildings, museums, and more.
- Offers an external booster antenna for use in the car, which allows me to have the PDA with me on the seat of the car while the antenna sits on the dash to get the best satellite signal.

On a recent trip to Atlanta the GPS took me all over the place, guiding me quite effectively through the many streets and taking me to a couple of cemeteries. While I was in the cemetery, it gave me GPS coordinates for the tombstones I found, so that the next time I have a chance to visit that cemetery I will not have to spend as much time searching for tombstones I want to return to. It also means I can share the coordinates online at sites such as Virtual Cemetery <www.genealogy.com> and Find-A-Grave <www.findagrave.com>.

A GPS FOR YOUR PDA?

GPS systems that are available for your PDA require a little homework. Before you settle on one, you first must determine if it will run on your PDA model and what requirements the GPS hardware has. For instance, my TeleType GPS uses the CompactFlash slot for the receiver. That means my PDA must have that type of a slot. The good news is that the manufacturers are very clear about which PDAs their products will work on and which ones require you to purchase any special accessories.

Once you have decided on a couple of potential candidates, check to see what points of interest they offer (such as cemeteries) and any other features you think are important, such as turn-by-turn directions or its ability to talk to you in a voice rather than communicating with text.

The following manufacturers all have systems designed to run on PDAs. This usually requires that you install software on your desktop or notebook computer, as that is where you download maps and other items from when planning a trip. The maps are usually so big that they cannot all fit on your PDA at once, unless you have purchased some large capacity media cards. But remember—if you only have one CompactFlash slot, you cannot save the maps there if that is where the GPS receiver has to go.

- Deluo <www.deluo.com>
- Mapopolis <www.mapopolis.com>
- Navman <www.navmanusa.com>
- Pharos <www.pharosgps.com>
- TeleType GPS <www.teletype.com>
- TomTom <www.tomtom.com>

JUST THE DIRECTIONS, PLEASE

If you have been to one of the online map sites such as MapQuest <www.mapquest.com> or MapBlast <www.mapblast.com> to get driving directions, you probably have printed them out and completely overlooked the option to save the directions and maps to your PDA. This way not only can you have the directions, but you also can use some turn-by-turn maps to orientate yourself as you are driving.

VIEWING PICTURES ON THE ROAD

There are times when I take digital pictures and I wish to view them with something a little larger than the two-inch LCD screen on my camera. With a PDA along that can handle the right cards, I have that opportunity. My digital camera saves images to an xD card and a CompactFlash card. Because the xD card takes less power from the batteries, most of my pictures end up on this small card. I discovered that I could get an adapter for the xD card and put it into the CompactFlash adapter, which then goes into my PDA.

With the included graphics viewer that comes with Pocket PC, it is easy enough to view the images. In fact, you can view any photo image. For instance, after using the small, battery-operated scanner discussed in chapter seven, I can pop the CompactFlash card out of the scanner, put it into my PDA, and view the images I've scanned.

Of course, there are more software options for viewing photos on a PDA than the one that may come with it.

- Album To Go (Palm OS) <www.clubphoto.com/tools/atg.php>
- dsPhoto Viewer (Pocket PC) <www.dreameesoft.com>
- Handmark PDA Photo (Palm OS) <www.handmark.com/products/pda photo>
- Photo Explorer (Pocket PC) <www.aidem.com.tw/English/index_englis h.htm>
- Photogather for Palm (Palm OS) <www.eusoftware.com>
- PicturePerfect (Pocket PC) <www.applian.com/pocketpc/pictureperfect>
- Picture Viewer (Pocket PC) <www.resco-net.com/picview.asp>
- Pocket Album (Pocket PC) <www.conduits.com/products/album>
- PocketPhoto (Palm OS) <www.dreamhs.com>
- SplashPhoto (Palm OS) <www.splashdata.com/splashphoto>

JUST THE BEGINNING

PDAs continue to evolve. Even now we are seeing a marriage between PDAs and cell phones. The addition of wireless methods of connection, such as Bluetooth, further connect the PDA to a separate phone if you still prefer to have your cell phone separate from your PDA.

Microtechnology continues to make things smaller. We are seeing things like 4-GB CompactFlash cards, which are still quite expensive, but which indicate the direction this wonderful technology is going. And as genealogists, we just need to hold on and see where it takes us. The more we can take with us, the more we may be able to do. We are no longer limited in our research by being unable to carry our files or that four-inch-thick folder of family group sheets with us.

Of course, with all the digitization and sharing among peripherals such as your PDA, it is easy for your computer to get cluttered with the images you have scanned or the digital photos you have taken. Have no fear—there are means to help you wrangle that computer back into line.

Definitions

BLUETOOTH

Bluetooth is a wireless standard that allows portable devices to connect to and talk to each other or to other devices that support it. This includes some cell phones, desktop computers, and notebook computers. The distance between the two devices is quite limited. If your computer doesn't have Bluetooth, you may be able to purchase an adapter card. This is easier for a notebook, where you can get a PCMCIA card.

Definitions

GIGABYTE

A *gigabyte* (GB) is equal to one billion bytes. This is actually a simplification of the exact number of bytes in a gigabyte, as it has been rounded. Gigabytes indicate the size of a hard drive or other storage device.

THIRTEEN

Organizing Your Digitized Genealogy

O
rganization is a word that sends even the mildest of genealogists into hysteria. There is something about organizing our office that just seems so overwhelming; it seems beyond hope. Perhaps that is why the idea of organizing a computer seems even more ludicrous. There are any number of systems designed for organizing your papers and your office, but none of them even mentions what to do with all the files that accumulate on your computer. So we will look at what is involved in gaining control of your computer and its many files that store your digitized records, photos, memorabilia, and other resources.

LOGGING THOSE FILES

One of the easiest ways to keep track of where things end up on your computer is to create a log. I mentioned the research log earlier as a way to track where you are in your research, so that you avoid wasting time by repeating research that produced nothing. The file log serves a similar purpose by helping you avoid wasting time when trying to find a particular photograph or other digitized image.

Any word processing program can be used to create a simple images log. I like to use the built-in table creation feature to design many of my logs. All you need to do is tell the word processor how many columns and rows you need. When you get to the end of the last row and still want to add more entries to the log, usually pressing the TAB key will tell the word processor to add another row to the table.

One of the things that you may feel is missing from the sample log in Figure 13-1 on page 154 is the location of each file on the computer's hard drive. Once I have scanned each photograph and done any restoration necessary, I then save the files on media off of the computer, such as CDs or DVDs. The

Tip

Figure 13-1

A digitized images log is a good way to keep track of the files you are making and is easily created in any word processing program.

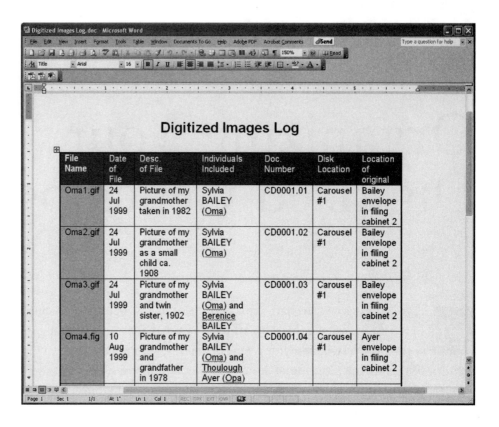

Digitized Images Log

File Name	Date of File	Desc. of File	Individuals Included	Doc. Number	Disk Location	Location of original
Oma1.gif	24 Jul 1999	Picture of my grandmother taken in 1982	Sylvia BAILEY (Oma)	CD0001.01	Carousel #1	Bailey envelope in filing cabinet 2
Oma2.gif	24 Jul 1999	Picture of my grandmother as a small child ca. 1908	Sylvia BAILEY (Oma)	CD0001.02	Carousel #1	Bailey envelope in filing cabinet 2
Oma3.gif	24 Jul 1999	Picture of my grandmother and twin sister, 1902	Sylvia BAILEY (Oma) and Berenice BAILEY	CD0001.03	Carousel #1	Bailey envelope in filing cabinet 2
Oma4.fig	10 Aug 1999	Picture of my grandmother and grandfather in 1978	Sylvia BAILEY (Oma) and Thoulough Ayer (Opa)	CD0001.04	Carousel #1	Ayer envelope in filing cabinet 2

For More Info

ME? MESSY?

Organization is important whether it is on your computer or in your office. A couple of useful books on organization include Sharon DeBartolo Carmack's *Organizing Your Family History Search* (Cincinnati: Betterway Books, 1999) and William Dollarhide's *Managing a Genealogical Project*, updated edition (Baltimore: Genealogical Publishing Company, 1999).

log reflects the location of the CDs by identifying them by number and location in my office.

If you plan to store your files on your computer, then you should list their exact locations in your log. That may look something like:

C:\my documents\my pictures\bahama trip\hopetown

With an exact path to the location of the file, you shouldn't have any trouble finding it later on. This assumes that you do keep the log and that you print it out, in addition to having it on your computer.

You may want to have more than one log, as well. The first would be a temporary log of sorts that lets you easily find any picture you have stored on your system at any given time. The second one would be for tracking the "permanent" storage of your images.

IS IT REALLY "PERMANENT?"

I put the word *permanent* in quotation marks above for a reason. As we discussed in the previous chapter, while CDs are estimated to last one hundred years, this is not always the case when they are subjected to everyday wear and tear.

So, while I burn my images onto compact discs, I also store them all on another medium as well. This may mean they are on a hard drive of another

> ## BACK UP, BACK UP, BACK UP
>
> If you want to ensure that you can always access your genealogical data, then you need to get in the habit of backing it up. This can be done in a number of different ways. You could copy files to Zip disks (they hold either 100 MB or 250 MB, depending on the drive you have). You could burn the information to compact disc or DVD if you have the necessary burner. You also could purchase an external hard drive, such as one of the Iomega HDD drives <www.iomega.com>.
>
> You may want to look into an off-site storage facility. Such facilities are usually accessed via the Internet and allow you to upload a certain amount of disk space for a fee. One that is devoted to genealogists is Genfolder <www.genfolder.com>.
>
> You may even want to make a practice of using more than one method of backing up. You can never be too careful when it comes to your data.

computer, or I have uploaded to them to a Web site storage area. Tape backup units are another option, though as we have seen with audio and videotapes, they eventually break down as well. Tape backup units can be installed into your computer or set on your desk, connected to the computer by a cable. Special tapes are used to "record" copies of your files for backing them up.

The key to permanence with images is to upgrade them to the next level of storage device as it becomes available. A few years ago I would not have dreamed it was possible to burn my own data DVDs, and yet DVD burners are now affordable enough for the average consumer to own. I am sure within a few years that there will be yet another medium that will hold even more files.

Important

ITEMS FOR YOUR LOG

If you create the log using a word processing program or a spreadsheet, then there is no limit to the information that you can store there. Remember that the point of the log is to identify the digitized files you want when you need them. In order to do that, you need to actually be able to navigate the log. So while you could include any number of columns, if each entry is too elaborate, then it is likely that you will be unable to quickly locate file names in the log, and that defeats the purpose. With that said, there are some things that should be considered when creating your log:

- *Name of the file*—the name of the electronic file, complete with the file extension.
- *Date of the file*—the date that I created the electronic file lets me know

---

PICKING THE BEST CD FOR THE JOB

When it comes to burning your own CDs, it is easy to pick up the wrong CDs and find out, a couple of years down the road, that you really don't have access to the files you thought you did. Many institutions that are backing up data or using CDs in a preservation mode use CD-R discs—that is, the gold, single-write discs. CD-R discs are supposed to be a better quality and more stable.

These are not the ones that you purchase a hundred at a time for five dollars. You are looking for a premium quality CD-R.

You also don't want to use the CD-RW, which stands for rewritable, discs for your preservation projects. Rewritable discs are designed to break down. In fact, as the burner is rewriting the disc that is what it does; it breaks down the medium so that it can write to it again. This is not the type of compact disc that you want to use for anything that you are expecting to last for any period of time on that CD.

Most manufacturers claim that a CD will last for one hundred years. Perhaps this is true in a perfect world of model weather and humidity conditions, but we all live in the real world, and your CD mileage will vary. Spend a little extra money on the good compact discs when it matters.

---

how old the file is and if I need to consider updating it.

- *Description of the file*—a brief but detailed description of the picture, tombstone, record, or other resource. I include the dates when the picture was taken whenever I know them.
- *Individuals included*—ideally, list the names of everyone in the picture, including the women's maiden names, if known. I also like to include any nicknames in parenthesis to more thoroughly identify them.
- *Document number*—this is a peculiarity of mine. I have always used document numbers in my research files as page numbers. I use them in the log to be able to "re-sort" the log based on the document number column's data. There are times when I rearrange the log by file name or something else. Notice that, in the sample from my log in Figure 13-1 on page 154, the document number goes up sequentially, based on the CD on which the files are found. As I start another CD, I go back to ".01" in the numbering.
- *File disk/disc location*—is for recording the physical location of the computer desktop folder, CD, DVD, or other medium on which the file is stored. This could be a CD tower, a rotating carousel, or a file folder. As long as you can look at the entry and know exactly where in your office you would find that disc, then you are fine.

- *Location of original*—this is the physical location of the original photograph, map, document, or other item. You never know when you may have to rescan or take another digital picture. Knowing who had the photograph last or what cemetery the tombstone was in (perhaps including GPS coordinates that you got with your PDA or other GPS) makes it easier to get another copy of it.

These are just some suggestions of what and why you might want to include particular categories of information in your log. You may find additional items important, such as the size of the file. Remember, as long as you include the extension of the file in its name, you will always know what kind of an image it is and what program you may need to use to open it. You may even find when you are creating your log that you have the same picture in different formats, so a notation of a high-resolution format or a Web version might be useful as well.

PUT THEM WITH THE FAMILY

Another method of organizing your images is to create separate compact discs of just those images pertinent to a particular family. This way, as you are researching a family and pull the appropriate files out of your filing cabinet, you will already have the images right there (see Figure 13-2 below).

You may still want to create an individual log to make it locating a single image quicker, but with the Windows Thumbnail view in Windows Explorer, you can get a small glimpse of all of the images, which makes it easier to find and open just the one you wanted.

Idea Generator

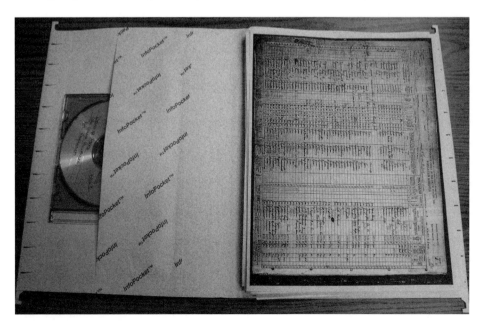

Figure 13-2
If you have digitized a lot of images pertinent to a particular family, you might consider putting a CD of those photos in the file for that family.

While you could use the Windows Explorer to view all of your images no matter where they are on your computer, you first need to know where you saved them, and that is usually the biggest problem; thus the logs. There is another alternative, however, if you do want to keep the images on your computer. Just remember that the images are large in size and will eat up a lot of hard disk space.

PHOTO ALBUM PROGRAMS

The same companies that create some of the image-editing programs understand that some of us are now feeling a little overwhelmed by all the images we have stored in our computer. It is possible that, while you would love to create a log, you no longer remember every place on your hard drive that you stored images. Various Photo Album programs can help with this.

Programs like Picasa and Photoshop Album scan your hard drive and create albums of the images they find there (see Figure 13-3 below). The organization of the images may vary from program to program. For instance, one of the software programs will group them all together, while another will arrange them by year or subject. Most of them allow you to attach keywords to the images so that at a later date you can use those keywords when searching for specific images.

Unlike some of the image-editing programs, most of the photo album applications are reasonably priced. Of course, just because they have a better

Figure 13-3

Picasa is a photo album program that will list all of the digitized images found on your hard drive, so it is easy to locate the ones that you want.

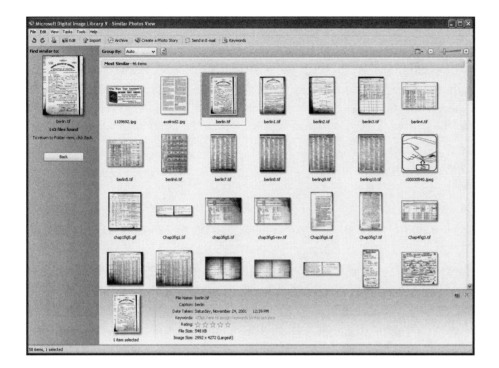

Figure 13-4
With Microsoft's Digital Image Library, you can tell the program to find images on your computer similar to the one selected.

price tag does not mean that you will want to purchase more than one. Knowing about the different features each one offers may help you better narrow it down to just one.

The ability to tag or otherwise link a *keyword* to an image makes searching much simpler down the road. Keywords can be anything you think is important, such as names of individuals in the photo or the location at which the photo was taken. Another interesting feature that you may find in e-photo albums is the ability to select an image and tell the software to find similar items. It then looks at the photos, compares them to the original, and displays a list of potentially similar images. This is a great time saver if you are looking for all the census scans you have on your computer, for instance (see Figure 13-4 above).

Tip

PHOTO ALBUM SOFTWARE PROGRAMS

These photo album software programs help you organize the many digitized images on your computer.

- 3D-Album <www.3d-album.com>

- Adobe Photoshop Album <www.adobe.com>

- I Image Library (part of the Digital Image Suite) <www.microsoft.com> Picasa <www.lifescapeinc.com/picasa>

- Virtual Album <www.albumsoftware.com>

EDITING THE PICTURE

Most photo album programs offer some basic editing features. Most of them limit the editing to a single image at a time, but a few allow you to select a batch of images to edit. Almost all of the photo album programs let you do the following simple changes:

- Adjust color
- Adjust tint
- Remove red-eye
- Crop
- Apply filters
- Rotate images

Photo album programs such as Microsoft's Digital Image Library and Adobe's Photoshop Album include menu options for launching their more powerful image-editing programs from within the albums, as well. As you are working in an album and you notice that one of the images needs more than basic editing, you will find that, provided you have installed either Adobe's Photoshop or Photoshop Elements or Microsoft's Digital Image Pro, you can do advanced editing of the images.

I WANT TO ARCHIVE THEM

An important feature in any photo album software should be the ability to create CDs and, if you have the hardware installed, DVDs. You should be able to pick up any photo album software box at the computer store and see this mentioned on the back. Storing images on CDs is a popular way of saving them so they don't take over your hard drive. Of course, once you move them to a CD, then your photo album software may only know about them if you have that disc in your CD-ROM drive.

HELP, I NEED A BIGGER HARD DRIVE

All of this storing and editing of images on your hard drive can quickly fill it up, especially if you are also digitizing your video and audio files. A long time ago we used to think that a 20-megabyte hard drive was top of the line and that we would never fill it up. How young and naïve we were. Now we find ourselves purchasing 40- and 80-gigabyte drives and still feeling the crunch. Why? A number of reasons.

First, our software programs take up a lot more space than they used to. For instance, to install Microsoft Digital Image Suite (which, as we discussed earlier, allows me to edit and organize my images), the system requirements

Reminder

warn me that I need to have at least 400 MB of available hard disk space. Think about that for a moment—twenty times the size of that 20 MB hard drive of yesteryear.

Add to that all of the images you have digitized using a camera or a scanner, and you begin to see how easy it is to fill up the hard drive. Now throw in a few video files, and you are bursting at the seams. This is one of the reasons I suggest storing your files off of the hard drive, to be put there only when you need them for a project. If you have digitized all your photos, you probably did so in an effort to preserve and restore them. Now that you have done that you only need to access a few of them at a time, perhaps as you create a new family history Web page or design a slide show for the upcoming family reunion. In the meantime those images need not be sitting on your hard drive if you need the room.

You can always purchase a bigger hard drive. Some systems can support more than one hard drive inside. This is certainly a good option, as it gives you lots of space, and you could reserve the second hard drive exclusively for images, putting no programs on it. If you can only put one hard drive in your system, then you have to weigh the time and energy involved in moving your files from the interior hard drive to the exterior. If you are not technologically savvy, this may mean taking the system to a computer shop to have the work done—costing you money and time.

There are a few devices I have already mentioned, but that I have not talked about in any detail. So let's take a moment to look at some of them.

CD-R AND CD-RW DISCS

Almost all computers now come with at the very least a CD-R drive—that is, a CD-ROM drive that allows you to write to a disk once. Most new systems come with CD-RW—that is, rewritable—drives as standard, and you may even find you can upgrade to a DVD writer for just a couple hundred dollars more.

CD-R discs are designed to be written to one time; CD-RW discs are designed to be written to more than once. The method in which the discs are rewritten makes the media less stable, so I don't recommend using CD-RW discs for long-term storage of your images. The medium is designed to break down, and that is not what we want to happen when our family photos are stored on them. And as I mentioned earlier in this chapter, when you really want them to last, invest the money in the high-end gold compact discs.

Tip

DVDS

DVD burners have come down in price throughout the last couple of years, making them affordable to hobbyists of all interests. **For genealogists, DVD**

burners let us create family movies on DVD, but they also can be used to store data. Think about it—a DVD-R can store about 4 GB of data, almost six times the capability of a CD-R. That's a lot of pictures.

You will find that many programs, such as Roxio's Easy CD & DVD Creator, recognize and write to DVDs if the hardware has been installed (see Figure 13-5 below). And as the name implies, these programs are designed to make writing to the DVD easy.

Figure 13-5
Roxio's Easy CD & DVD Creator will help you in creating discs of files, including your digital images and family stories.

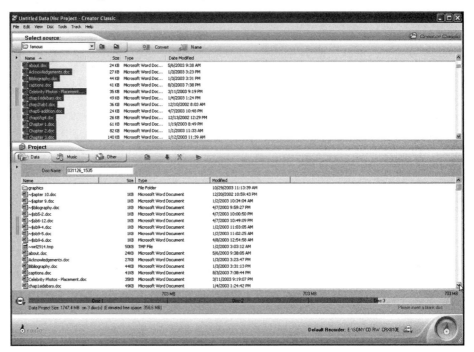

Just as I talked about with the compact disc options, it is better to burn onto a DVD-R rather than a DVD-RW disc. That is because, like we discussed with CD-Rs and CD-RWs, the discs that are designed to be written to only once do not break down as quickly as the rewritable ones do.

REMOVABLE DRIVES

Removable drives, such as the Zip (see Figure 13-6 on page 163), Jaz, or SyQuest drives, offer limited storage capacity, from as little as 100 MB to as much as 2 GB per disk. These drives often use modified floppy disks. However, they can be a great option in a pinch or when saving smaller files.

Not all of these drives will be an option. You may need to look around for an external drive—one that sits on your desk instead of being installed in your computer—to take full advantage of these storage techniques, depending on how full your computer is already. Those that can be connected via USB ports are my favorites. Windows recognizes the peripheral when it is hooked up, but I don't have to keep it hooked up, and this gives me flexibility.

Figure 13-6
You may also find a Zip drive useful for saving a few digital files at a time.

Another removable drive, while designed for backing up data and disaster recovery, is something like the Iomega HDD drives <www.iomega.com>. Such drives come in sizes from 20 to 250 gigabytes of storage space, and can be connected to your computer through USB or FireWire. If your computer has FireWire, then I strongly suggest you use it—it's much faster.

TAPE BACKUP SYSTEMS

I don't actually recommend these for the storage of your images for long periods of time. What I do recommend a tape backup system for is to do just what it says—to back up your system. There is nothing worse than going to boot up your computer only to find out that it has taken an unscheduled vacation. It's like going to a store and finding the "Gone Fishing" sign hanging in the window for days. You never know if the owner is going to come back and open up. When your computer crashes, you never know just what information you can retrieve from it and how much it will cost to do it.

If you are routinely backing up your system to tape, then you will find that you have no worries. Good tape backup systems actually do two things. You can set them up to back up your entire system, perhaps once a month, and then do interim backups once a week, or once a night, of files that have changed in that time period. The idea is that, should your computer crash, you will not have lost anything.

Tip

CONSIDER UPGRADING YOUR DATA DISCS

If you purchase a DVD burner, especially if you get one that is going to sit on your desk rather than replace your CD drive, then you may want to make a point of migrating the data from your CDs to DVDs. The good news is that you can fit about four CDs to one DVD, so you'll have fewer discs to keep track of.

Warning

Definitions

MAGNETO-OPTICAL DRIVE

A *magneto-optical drive* gives you sort of the best of both worlds. It uses the magnetic properties of traditional disk drives, like floppy disk drives, along with the high storage capability of CD-ROMs. These drives are not as popular in the United States as they are in Asia. While they have qualities of both the magnetic and CD-ROM drives, they are also faster at accessing data than either of the other drives are.

If you have images on your system at the time of the backup, then they will be put on the tape, but finding things on a tape is not always as easy or as quick as popping a CD in and opening right to the image you want. The tape drives, after all, work just as your old audiotape recorders and players did. In order to find a specific song, it was necessary to fast-forward or rewind until you got to the right spot. The same thing takes place on a tape backup system.

NO GUARANTEES?

You may feel like there are no guarantees when it comes to your digitized images. While I often stress when I am lecturing that it is not *if* but *when* your computer will crash, most of the time, if you have saved things on one or more of the various drives and media discussed earlier, you will find that you have maintained everything you had on the computer before the unexpected technical difficulties.

Actually, most of what was discussed in the latter part of this chapter applies to everything on your computer, from your e-mail to your genealogy program files to your word processing program documents. Computers are wonderful tools, but there are a few uncertainties that come with them. All we can do is our best to foresee problems and head them off. Backing up files to tape and other media is just one of the ways in which we can do this.

Keeping paper copies is another way. One of the reasons I have that column in the digitized image log about the location of the original is so that if something happens I know where to turn to hopefully get another digitized image. So why bother digitizing in the first place? Preservation, among other things. If you can use the digitized image instead of constantly pulling out the original document, then the originals have a chance of lasting much longer, provided they are being properly stored.

Anything that helps me preserve originals and reach out to family members, even when it comes with a few potential problems, seems to me to be a win-win situation.

FOURTEEN

Coming Full Circle

T hroughout this book we have looked at all the many different ways you can use your computer, with various peripherals and the latest technology, to enhance and preserve your genealogy. All of the different ways you can embrace technology should not detract from your genealogical pursuits, but instead should augment that research.

Each generation that we identify brings with it new questions. Each new generation also brings with it double the names we are looking for. Genealogy software helps you to maintain an order to those individuals by placing them in family units. As you begin to digitize photographs and documents, you will find that you can link them to the individuals in your genealogy database.

Of course, as we have seen, there are many other ways you can use the computer with a variety of peripherals to not only track but preserve your family history. Think of all of the documents that you can save in electronic formats, offering you a chance to print them out whenever you need them, or to share via e-mail with other cousins around the country or the world. No longer must you make a copy of the original each time someone asks you. Now you truly can protect those originals so that they will still be around a hundred years from now for your descendants.

Back in Touch

Perhaps one of the things I find most interesting about digitizing the photos and documents that I have, especially when I first began, is the re-introduction I received to my ancestors and the research I had done about them. **With a new eye, or simply just a fresh eye, there were times that I read the documents and thought of new research angles.** Other times going through a family file has reinvigorated my interest in researching that particular line again.

There is something about using your scanner and having to really look at

Tip

the images you are capturing that forces you to actually see what is there. After all, as you are scanning a document and you see it on the screen, you want to make sure the entire document is readable before moving on to the next image. As such, you may be reading through the digitized document and seeing the whole thing for the first time. Too often we skim the photocopies we make, running the risk of missing valuable clues.

Of course, this approach does take longer during the scanning process, since I am not just using a sheetfed scanner to process many images quickly. It takes me longer to get all my documents digitized, but that's okay with me.

I've been researching my family for more than twenty years, and I have a select family file of about three thousand individuals. Each of those people has been proven to be related beyond a doubt before he or she was added to my database. I am not impressed with numbers. Those who claim they have been researching for a year and now have sixty thousand names in their database don't know fifty-nine thousand of them—not really. Genealogy isn't about numbers, at least not in how many names you can get in the shortest amount of time. Instead it is about family and knowing that the individuals you have in your database are indeed members of that family (see Figure 14-1 below).

Figure 14-1
Genealogy programs now do more than just show you your families.

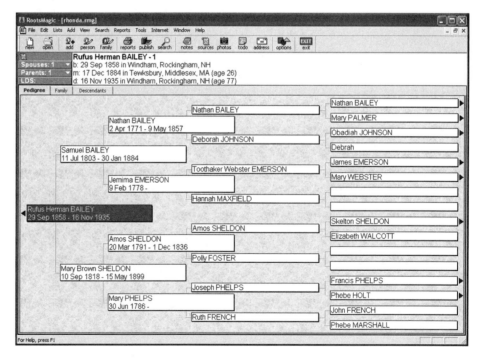

My opinion about genealogy has also colored my approach to digitizing photos, documents, and heirlooms. I take pride in the final file. As a result, I am willing to concede that it will take me more time to get everything eventually digitized. I never know when I might want to use one of the records for a lecture, feature it in a book, or publish it to my Web site. By taking my time during the initial scanning, I eventually save time in the final editing of that image, in some instances never even having to edit it at all.

NO LIMITS

Once you have digitized photographs and documents, you can publish these not only on CDs for family and friends, but also on the Internet. Reaching out to other cousins via your online creation will bring you contacts you may never have reached through more traditional publishing methods. And there are many other ways you can use what is on your computer, especially if you have a PDA.

You now know that not only can you use the genealogy software programs designed for personal digital assistants to take your entire database with you, but some of them even offer you the opportunity to record notes about what you find when you are in the research field. Instead of having to take along lots of files or lug your notebook computer—which, while portable, is not always appropriate—you could use the PDA. **In some research libraries, I have used just my PDA with the portable keyboard designed to work with it to gather notes from resources that I am not allowed to photocopy or scan, especially when it is inconvenient to use my notebook** (see Figure 14-2 below).

Tip

Figure 14-2
A full-sized keyboard can make entry into a PDA much easier when you are researching.

CHECKING IMAGES ON THE ROAD

Recently when I was in Wisconsin to lecture, the host was kind enough to let me visit the Wisconsin State Historical Society. I have a penchant for old newspapers, so I was soon ensconced on a reader, happily getting lost in the

Waupaca County Republican from the year 1886. Because I was giving a lecture on scanners at that seminar, I wanted to add something unique to my presentation. As I was reading the newspapers and making photocopies from the microfilms, I decided I would use my portable HP Photosmart 1200 scanner to digitize some of the articles in the newspaper, which I could then add to the lecture.

As I was scanning them, they were saved to a CompactFlash card, which I then popped into my PDA to view. There was no sense in powering up my notebook until I had the images I wanted. So using the PDA to view those images allowed me to quickly scan and then double-check the results (see Figure 14-3 below).

Figure 14-3
Using the Pictures program on the Pocket PC is a quick way to check the scans I did of an 1886 newspaper.

Now consider this possibility: Provided your PDA has an expansion slot so that you can use one of the media cards discussed in chapter twelve, you could load up some of your images and take them to the family reunion to show folks. In fact, PDAs now offer a slideshow feature, so you could create a folder of images that would then just rotate through on their own.

Not only could you have your genealogy in a condensed version, but you also could take along many of the images that you might need to refer to while on the road. Perhaps your family members even could make their own copies from you right on the spot, provided their computers could handle the type of media card on which you had them stored.

NEVER BE STUCK AGAIN

Too often when I am at the Family History Library I overhear a patron bemoaning the fact that she has hit a serious brick wall on the lineage she brought with her, but hasn't brought anything else to work on and still has three days left of her trip. If there is one thing that we don't want to do, it's waste time when we are at any major repository. It costs us too much in money and time to squander even a minute.

If you have digitized your files that now sit at home and have your genealogy either in a PDA or on a notebook computer, then you are not limited. You can pick up the research of any of your other lines, especially if you also have the research logs of your past endeavors either as scanned images or in a word processing document. I try to make sure that I have everything I might need on CompactFlash or SD cards before I head out, especially if I'm headed somewhere that I will not be taking my notebook computer.

In some repositories I may be able to use my camera or my scanner, thus cutting down on the costs of photocopies. Remember, though, to check ahead of time with the repository. There's no sense bringing things you can't use. More and more we are finding each venue's rules regarding such things available on the Web sites of the repositories we want to visit. But if they haven't posted anything about what you can and cannot bring into the repository, or if you are hoping you can use a scanner, it is best to phone ahead.

Money Saver

I remember visiting the Margaret Herrick Library in Los Angeles on a research trip when I was compiling some celebrity family trees. They were understandably quite protective of their records and books. You were limited to your papers, something to write with, and, if you had it, you could take your laptop or PDA, as well. Everything else had to be put in a locker. To help cut down on the costs of photocopies—and the time it took to get them, as the staff made all copies—I used my notebook computer to extract pertinent family details. Now that I have a more advanced PDA, I would be able to use it in the same capacity with the small keyboard, making my arrival at the library a little less like I was trying to run away from home with my PDA and keyboard tucked nicely into a small purse. Also, it would save me time when I was ready to leave the library, as they would not need to have me open the notebook to verify I hadn't secreted any documents away in the computer.

With all the technology we have at our fingertips, there really is no limit to what we might accomplish, how we might do it, and what we can make easier for ourselves when we head home with all our new treasures. Just remember that part of preservation also extends to the files you now have on your various devices.

DON'T FORGET TO BACK UP

I remember a particularly blustery day about ten years ago. Each time the wind kicked up, the power in my house dipped just enough to take my desktop computer offline. It was obvious there was a loose wire or something outside, so I decided to call the city and report the problem. The response I received took me aback for a moment, when the lady who answered the phone told me, "Well, dearie, when dealing with large machines such as those we have here, you have to expect some problems."

At that point I decided that I would need to be proactive in the protecting of my computer, and I invested in a universal power supply (UPS) so that if the power dipped my computer would not feel it. It has saved me a number of times since then, and I consider it a wise investment.

Backing up our files, especially our genealogy files, which are usually one of a kind, is also a wise investment in time, money, and effort. You would be devastated if you flipped on your computer only to discover that the hard drive wasn't booting up. I know, you are sitting there saying you have a new computer, less than a year old, it won't happen to you. Remember it is not *if* but *when* your computer will decide to act up. And I have found that it chooses the most inopportune times to do so.

Warning

Even if you have all your photographs burned to CDs or DVDs, remember that those are not always infallible, and they do have shelf lives. You always can rescan pictures and documents you own. But if you are dealing with something that practically cost you an arm and a leg to procure from cousin Maggie, then you definitely want that image to last on your computer. Having it in multiple forms—on your hard drive, on a CD, on a tape backup or external hard drive—helps to ensure the likelihood that when you want it, it will still be available.

REMEMBER TO BE COURTEOUS

We are almost to the end of our time together, and I do feel that being courteous when using any of your electronic gadgets is of utmost importance. Sometimes we get so wrapped up in what we are doing that we forget how it might affect those around us.

What sounds quiet and soft when you are in your house—with the television going and your daughter or grandson talking on the phone—is quite a bit louder in a hushed library. The beeping of a camera or the "enhanced" sounds that some digital cameras use to simulate the sounds of a traditional camera may not seem disruptive, until the person next to you is trying to concentrate on deciphering chicken scratch that is hiding under the guise of seventeenth century handwriting.

If you are using your PDA or notebook computer, remember to mute the sounds. Most of the programs make some noises as they are launching or when a message box opens. While those noises are fine in the comfort of your home, they are not necessary when you are at the library. The next time you visit your library listen to how often you hear the songs of notebooks booting up. You'll see what I mean.

A FEW FINAL THOUGHTS

I am always on the lookout for the latest gadgets that are coming along. I suppose this is the geek in me peaking out. But as I am reading computer magazines or checking out products at the computer store or online, I am also looking at how they can help me with my genealogy. Sometimes that benefit doesn't come immediately to mind, especially when we are trying to apply twentieth century thinking to twenty-first century technology. But I know that when I first got my PDA, I used it only for keeping track of my appointments. Now I use it all the time. When I am at my desk, it sits beside me within easy view and reach. When I am on the road, it is one of the first things I make sure I have with me.

I can say the same now when it comes to my small scanner. I like having it with me. While I shared the story of lecturing in Wisconsin and scanning on the fly, there were many times before I got it when I had wished for that very ability. We are almost in an "ask and ye shall receive" time, and I can't wait to see what we ask for next to help us with our hunt for ancestors.

WALK THROUGH THE DOOR AND
LET THE ADVENTURE BEGIN

Computers and technology really have progressed, and the new products and features that appear continue to astound me. As you are deciding on a scanner or buying your first digital camera, remember that you will need to have a little patience as you learn how best to use each new gadget.

In introducing you to how you can digitize your family history, I have opened the door for you so that you could get a glimpse of what is possible. It is now up to you to take what you have seen and make it truly your own. Enjoy the adventure.

Glossary of Terms

ARM: Advanced RISC Machine. A processor chip used in many portable devices, including PDAs, because it is powerful, inexpensive to make, and doesn't generate a lot of heat. In PDAs, this may determine what software you can install on your palm-sized PC.

bit rate: The number of colors the hardware can handle. Displayed as 16-bit or 48-bit, it lets you know the number of bits used for each pixel. A 16-bit color depth means the hardware can handle 16.7 million colors. See color depth.

bluetooth: A short-range wireless method of connecting devices for data transfer, such as connecting a PDA to a notebook computer to synchronize addresses, tasks, and appointments.

BMP: Bit map. A file format used for graphics such as wallpaper in Microsoft Windows.

CCD: Charge-coupled device. Digital cameras, camcorders, and scanners use this special arrangement of semiconductors, in which the output of the one semiconductor leads into the input of the next semiconductor.

CD-ROM: Compact disc with read-only memory. A CD can hold approximately 650 MB of data, or approximately 300,000 pages of text.

citation: The formal notation of a source of information.

clipboard: A memory feature that Microsoft Windows uses to store the last information that a user copied or cut (but did not delete). It is useful when transferring information or files from one place to another, such as from the media card of a digital camera to the hard drive of the computer.

color depth: The number of colors the hardware can handle. Displayed as 16-bit or 48-bit, it lets you know the number of bits used for each pixel. A 16-bit color depth means the hardware can handle 16.7 million colors. See bit rate.

Compact Flash: A removable storage device, also known as flash memory, used in such portable devices as PDAs and digital cameras.

compression: Data compression is any method of condensing digital information so that it can be stored in a smaller file, and is thus transferable more quickly.

copyright: Offers protection to authors, artists, musicians, and others to help encourage them in their creative endeavors. This is done by limiting what others may do with the works covered by copyright.

database: A searchable, compiled, and computerized list.

decode: The act of putting the file in a form that the computer can recognize.

directories: The sub-folders or divisions found on the hard drive, CD-ROM, DVD, or media card into which files are saved. More often referred to as folders in Windows.

download: To receive a file sent from another computer via modem, cable modem, wireless, or other connection. *Download* is synonymous with *receive.*

DPI: Dots per inch. Indicates the resolution of the scanner, printer, camera, or image itself. The higher the number, the sharper the image.

DV: Digital video. A full-motion video that has been converted to a binary file recognized by the computer.

DVD: Digital versatile disc. A CD-like disc with an extremely high capacity, allowing the storage of 4.7 gigabytes of data, or a full-length feature film.

DVD writer: A hardware device that allows you to create your own DVDs. See DVD.

encode: The act of changing something to a programming code, such as the conversion of an analog videotape into a digital file.

export: To transfer data from one computer to another or from one application to another. See import.

family group sheet: A form that includes vital information on a father, mother, and children in a given family.

FireWire: The name Apple gave to the IEEE 1394, a cable connection that transfers data at a high rate, making it good for moving digitized graphics and digitizing analog video.

Flash memory: A type of memory that writes or rewrites in blocks of data rather than byte by byte, allowing the file or image to be saved more quickly.

flatbed scanner: A scanner that offers a flat glass plate upon which to place an item for scanning. Flatbed scanners are especially useful when working with bound volumes and fragile photographs.

FPS: Frames per second. The speed at which video moves from one frame to the next, thus showing a moving picture.

gamma settings: The relationship between the input levels of the scanner and the output levels. Adjusting the gamma settings when possible in your scanner software is more precise than working with the brightness and contrast options when a scan appears darker or lighter than it should.

GIF: Graphic interchange format. A bit-map color graphics file format that is widely used in HTML documents for images.

gigabyte: Commonly written as GB or *gig*, this term is used to describe the size of storage of a hard drive, tape, or DVD and is approximately 1 billion bytes.

GPS: Global positioning satellite. A method of determining your location by using the input from satellites through a receiver and special software that gives you longitude and latitude coordinates and shows that position on a map.

handheld scanner: A scanner that can be held in your hand. It moves across the page as you move your hand across a page. It may require that you make multiple passes of the document, and then stitch those images together using graphics software.

import: To bring a file created in one application or system into another application or system. See export.

inkjet printer: A printer that uses liquid ink sprayed on the page to print. These are seldom waterproof, but offer an inexpensive way to print in color. Current printers offer high-quality output and may use both a black cartridge as well as a color cartridge.

Internet: A noncommercial, self-governing network devoted mostly to communication and research, with millions of uses worldwide. The Internet is not a service and has no real central hub. Rather, it is a collection of tens of thousands of networks, online services, and single-user computers.

interpolation: A method of enhancing the actual resolution of an image by duplicating pixels to double or triple the pixels per inch. Scanners and some digital cameras may give the resolutions listed as actual and with interpolation.

JPEG: Joint photographic expert group. Often used in discussing the .jpg file format that uses a compression technique to reduce the size of a graphics file. Many digital cameras use this file format as the default when saving images.

laser printer: A printer that uses a black powder, toner, that sticks to the page after the page has been heated. Laser printers offer high-quality results and now come in black and white as well as color versions.

macro feature: In a digital camera, it allows the camera's lens to be physically close (sometimes within an inch or less) to the item being photographed without losing focus.

megabyte: Commonly referred to as MB or *meg*, this is a unit of file storage that is equivalent to 1,048,576 bytes.

megapixel: One megapixel is equivalent to 1,048,576 pixels.

Memory stick: Sony's proprietary memory card resembling a small stick of chewing gum that is used in many of the Sony digital products, including their Palm products and digital cameras.

Micro drive: A hard drive that is the size of a Compact Flash card, but that has file storage in gigabytes. See Compact Flash.

MiniDV: A tape designed for the latest digital video cameras. It records video in a digital format that is recognized by computers.

MIPS: Multiprocessor without interlocked pipeline stages. This type of processor is used in palm-sized devices because of its small size and low power consumption.

MMC: MultiMediaCard. One of the flash memory cards used by portable devices like digital cameras and PDAs. An MMC card can be used in an SD slot, but an SD card cannot be used in an MMC slot. See SD.

MP3: Moving pictures expert group audio layer three. It borrows the sound layer of the MPEG video file format, which allows it to compress the audio file to one-twelfth its original size. It is a popular format for music, and you can find special devices designed to hold and play many songs in this format. See MPEG.

MPEG: Moving pictures expert group. A video compression standard that computers use to create and show video.

MPEG4: Moving pictures expert group-4. The latest standard for video on computers, it is the successor to MPEG-1 and MPEG-2 (there was no MPEG-3). It is primarily designed for low-bandwidth systems such as wireless devices.

native format: The preferred file type used by your graphics software.

OCR: Optical character recognition. Built into many scanning software programs, it allows you to scan a typed page and convert it to a text file that can then be edited using any text or word processing program.

online: Refers to the successful connection with another computer via a modem, cable line, or network.

orientation: Refers to the position of the page. Page orientation can be portrait (vertical) or landscape (horizontal).

PCX: A graphics file format.

PDA: Personal digital assistant. A palm-sized PC that in the past had limited functionality, usually limited to recording of appointments, tasks, and notes. Today's devices offer many more features.

photo index sheet: A page printed by some photo printers that displays the photos on a digital media card, so you tell the printer which ones you want printed.

photo printer: A printer intended to print high-quality photos from a computer or a digital camera. Some of them now come with built-in card readers, allowing you to print without having the printer connected to a computer.

photo scanner: A scanner, usually of the flatbed variety, optimized for scanning photographs as opposed to pages of text.

point-and-click: A less expensive camera that does not require any manual focus or other adjustments, though it may have additional features.

PPI: Pixels per inch. Used interchangeably with dots per inch (dpi) when referring to resolution.

prosumer: A level of consumer product that is less expensive than a professional product, but is higher quality than a typical consumer would seek. With digital cameras, some 5- and 6-megapixel cameras fall into this category.

RAM: Random-access memory. Your computer puts information into RAM for easier and quicker access. This area can be written and rewritten to many times during a single session on the computer. This type of memory is easily expandable by adding chips to the motherboard. RAM is your computer's workspace.

RAW: As the name implies, this is an uncompressed image file that certain high-end digital cameras create that offers the photographer flexibility in working with that file, provided the graphics software can open the RAW file format.

resolution: Refers to the sharpness of an image. It is referenced when dealing with monitors, printers, and scanners. It is generally rated in dots per inch. The higher the dpi, the sharper the image.

RTF: Rich text format. A cross-platform, cross-application text-document format. It includes some, but not all, of the formatting information that is included in many word processing documents.

SD: Secure digital. One of the flash memory cards used by portable devices like PDAs and digital cameras. An SD card slot can hold either an SD card or an MMC card. See MMC.

serial port: A port on the computer that allows for the connection of a keyboard or modem. Your computer identifies these as communication (COM) ports and gives each one a number. Some systems have upwards of four of these.

sheet-fed scanner: A scanner that slides individual pages so that they pass over a stationary scanning head. Such a scanner can only work with sheets of paper, as opposed to with a bound volume.

SLR: Single-lens reflex. A type of camera in which what you see in the viewfinder is the same as what the camera sees. Digital SLR cameras are high-end professional cameras.

SmartMedia: The thinnest of the flash memory cards, used by portable devices like PDAs, digital cameras, and some MP3 players. May be replaced by xD cards. See xD.

TIFF: Tagged image file format. Represented by the file extension .tif, it is the file format used in prosumer and high-end digital cameras for picture perfect output.

transparency adapter: A peripheral device that attaches to a flatbed scanner and illuminates photo negatives and 35mm slides, allowing the scanner to digitize the object.

TWAIN: Originally thought to mean "technology without an interesting name," the term actually gets its meaning from "ne'er the twain shall meet." This is because the data source manager sits between the driver and the application. This has become the standard interface in scanning. Many graphics programs and some genealogy programs are TWAIN compatible.

upload: To transfer a file from a local computer to a remote host. *Upload* is synonymous with *transmit,* while *download* is synonymous with *receive.* See download.

USB: Universal serial bus. A cable connection that is replacing serial and parallel port connections on computers. It allows "hot swapping," so you could unplug your camera and plug in your scanner without having to reboot your computer. There are two standards—1.1 and 2.0. The 2.0 standard is faster, achieving transfer speeds as fast as those of FireWire. See FireWire.

user error: Something that we hate to admit. We will always blame the computer, scanner, printer, or program for any mishap before we admit that perhaps we are at fault. *User error* generally means we didn't type something in correctly or accurately tell the computer what we wanted in the first place. This is sometimes the result of unfamiliarity with the computer, the peripheral, or the program.

WAV: Windows audiovisual. Sound files that work with Microsoft Windows Media Player and Microsoft Windows Sound Recorder.

WMA: Windows media audio. A file format developed by Microsoft for music files that competes with the MP3 format. These are smaller files that offer security features to prevent copying and piracy. See MP3.

WMV: Windows media video. Microsoft's file format for storing digitized video. The files are smaller than MPEG files. See MPEG.

xD: Extreme digital. A flash memory card introduced by FujiFilm and Olympus. The smallest of all memory cards, it will likely replace SmartMedia cards. See SmartMedia.

Xscale: The latest ARM-based processor that is much faster than its predecessors while still being conservative of power, making it a great processor for use in such devices as PDAs. See ARM.

Index

More Books for the Genealogist From Family Tree Books!

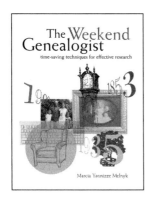

The Weekend Genealogist—Maximize your family research efficiency! With this guide, you can focus your efforts on searching for family documents and gain the best results. Organization and research techniques are presented in a clear, easy-to-follow format perfect for advanced researchers and beginners. You'll learn how to work more efficiently using family history facilities, the Internet—even the postal service!
ISBN 1-55870-546-5, paperback, 144 pages, #70496-K

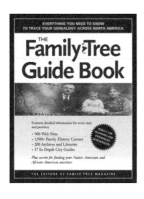

The Family Tree Guide Book—This invaluable resource—from the editors of *Family Tree Magazine*—combines genealogy basics, online directories, and region-specific travel information in one book. Divided into seven regions of the U.S. with a chapter covering Canada, each section introduces you to a specific region and provides guidelines for finding and using its records.
ISBN 1-55870-647-X, paperback, 352 pages, #70595-K

Your Guide to Cemetery Research—Cemeteries can help fill the holes in your precious family history! With this book, you'll learn how to determine when and where a person died, locate the exact cemetery in which a family or individual is interred, analyze headstones and markers, interpret funerary art and tombstone iconography, and more!
ISBN 1-55870-589-9, paperback, 192 pages, #70527-K

Genealogist's Computer Companion—Master the basics of online research and turn your computer into an efficient, versatile research tool. Respected genealogist Rhonda McClure shows you how, providing guidelines and advice that enable you to find new information, verify existing research, and save valuable time. She also provides an invaluable glossary of genealogical and technical terms.
ISBN 1-55870-591-0, paperback, 176 pages, #70529-K

Finding Your Roots Online—It's the guide you need to lead you through your online research! Nancy Hendrickson's structured, easy-to-follow approach covers the basics of sound genealogical research, and helps you navigate the Internet efficiently and effectively. Also included are pages of tips and techniques for organizing computer research that can make your online efforts easier, faster, and more productive.
ISBN 1-55870-635-6, paperback, 228 pages, #70583-K

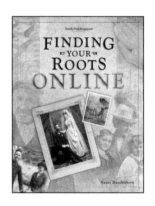

The Genealogist's Q&A Book—More than 150 answers to the most commonly asked questions are found here in a friendly, easy-to-browse format that will clarify the research process and save you time and confusion as you fill in your family tree. Questions are conveniently grouped according to the different resources you'll use: from census, church, and immigration records to oral histories, Web sites, electronic databases, and more.
ISBN 1-55870-590-2, paperback, 240 pages, #70528-K

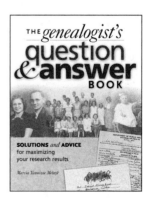

Your Guide to the Family History Library—The Family History Library in Salt Lake City is the largest collection of genealogy and family history materials in the world. No other repository compares for both quantity and quality of research materials. Written for beginning and intermediate genealogists, *Your Guide to the Family History Library* will help you use the library's resources effectively, both on-site and online.
ISBN 1-55870-578-3, paperback, 240 pages, #70513-K

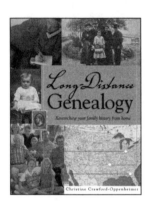

Long Distance Genealogy—Gathering information from sources that can't be visited is a challenge for all genealogists. This book will teach you the basics of long-distance research. You'll learn what types of records and publications can be accessed from a distance, problems associated with the process, how to network, how to use computer resources, and special "last resort" options.
ISBN 1-55870-535-X, paperback, 208 pages, #70495-K

Your Guide to the Federal Census—This one-of-a-kind book examines the "nuts and bolts" of census records. You'll find out where to view the census and how to use it to find ancestors quickly and easily. Easy-to-follow instructions and case studies detail nearly every scenario for tracing family histories through census records. You'll also find invaluable appendixes, a glossary of census terms, and extraction forms.
ISBN 1-55870-588-0, paperback, 192 pages, #70525-K